THE MONEY MAZE

NAVIGATE YOUR WAY THROUGH PERSONAL FINANCE IN THE UK

HOW TO MANAGE MONEY, PAY OFF DEBT & SAVE WELL

WILLIAM PRITCHARD

© Copyright – William Pritchard - 2022 - All rights reserved.

The content contained within this book may not be reproduced, duplicated, or transmitted without direct written permission from the author or the publisher.

Under no circumstances will any blame or legal responsibility be held against the publisher, or author, for any damages, reparation, or monetary loss due to the information contained within this book. Either directly or indirectly. You are responsible for your own choices, actions, and results.

Legal Notice:

This book is copyright protected. This book is only for personal use. You cannot amend, distribute, sell, use, quote or paraphrase any part, or the content within this book, without the consent of the author or publisher.

Disclaimer Notice:

Please note the information contained within this document is for educational and entertainment purposes only. All effort has been executed to present accurate, up to date, and reliable, complete information. No warranties of any kind are declared or implied. Readers acknowledge that the author is not engaging in the rendering of legal, financial, medical or professional advice. The content within this book has been derived from various sources.

Please consult a licensed professional before attempting any techniques outlined in this book.

By reading this document, the reader agrees that under no circumstances is the author responsible for any losses, direct or indirect, which are incurred as a result of the use of the information contained within this document, including, but not limited to, — errors, omissions, or inaccuracies.

TABLE OF CONTENTS

INTRODUCTION	**6**
CHAPTER ONE	**11**
Where Is My Money?	11
Assets, Liabilities, & Net Weath	11
CHAPTER TWO	**27**
Where Else Is My Money Kept?	27
Let's Talk Payslips & Pensions	27
CHAPTER THREE	**38**
Where Does My Money Go?	38
Taxes & Other Deductions	38
CHAPTER FOUR	**53**
What Should I Do Next?	53
Recording Expenses & Cutting Bills	53
CHAPTER FIVE	**74**
What About The Things I Just Have To Pay?	74
Saving On The Unavoidable Stuff	74

CHAPTER SIX   99

What To Do With What's Left?   99

A Bit On Budgeting   99

CHAPTER SEVEN   116

What To Do With All Your Extra Cash?   116

Debts & How To Repay Them   116

CHAPTER EIGHT   138

How & Where To Save?   138

Let's Talk About Accounts   138

CHAPTER NINE   159

How To Organise Your Finances   152

Different Accounts, Tracking Net Weath & Automation   152

CONCLUSION   157

REFERENCES   170

NOTES   178

INTRODUCTION

Let's take a brief journey into dreamland.

What does your dream life look like? Maybe, it's your kids playing around your table with a glass of Pinot Grigio in hand as you stare at the most beautiful woman on earth- who coincidentally happens to be your wife.

Or perhaps, it's you in the front seat of your new Lamborghini SUV, driving a couple of friends to La Gavroche, London, to have a totally bang average meal after a stress-free day of being your own boss…Stop.

Snapback out.

How did that feel? Thrilling? Exciting? Mouth-drooling?

Great, well, I want you to remember this when times get tough, and you feel like giving up.

Personal finance can be challenging, but when implemented correctly, everything you dream of can and will become a reality.

Look around; everyone has the potential to become whatever they truly desire to be. But then, what's the difference between the people who dream and those who succeed?

It's not determination.

Neither is it grit.

One word - **education**.

Let me put it this way- the game of wealth is not simply a game of numbers. Although the numbers are, of course fundamental, becoming wealthy requires much more.

But then, you know this already- right? You've been there before.

You may have even watched your parents argue about not having enough money as a kid.

So, you have a pretty good grip over how vital being financially intelligent is to your ambition to be a better parent, a better partner, or whatever it might be.

I was the same; I am the same. And in my searches to find the magical answer, the magic piece of information that would solve all my problems, all I actually found, were more bloody problems.

Problem one –

Almost EVERYTHING is geared towards U.S. audiences and financial systems! Can somebody please tell me what good learning to max out a 401k is, as a British teen?

Problem two –

Everyone tells you WHAT to do, but not HOW to do it. (And between you and me, knowing how is actually quite helpful).

And finally, I'll present you with:

Problem three –

Everything there is to know about a topic, is dumped on you, all at once and what? You're expected to walk away as a fully qualified financial advisor? I think not.

If even one of these problems has pissed you off as much as it did me, then you're in the right place.

In this book, we will be going on a journey with Lloyd. Our book's protagonist.

Lloyd is an employee of a U.K. based company, earning £20,000 a year. Unfortunately, Lloyd is also in a bit of debt and has far too many outgoings each month.

Lloyd will be carrying out everything that we mention in this book, and here's the best bit.

Everything he does will be shown to you. All you then need to do is copy Lloyd with your own personal finances, and by the end of it…

Well, you'll be well on your way to whatever you dreamed of earlier.

Sound good?

Great. But, how do we actually get there?

It all starts with building a sturdy foundation. Only when we have an unbreakable base, can we begin to scale the path of becoming wealthy.

We only get one chance in this life. So why not spend it at the top, experiencing the most amazing things, than to be at the bottom, struggling to meet basic needs.

So, what does a good foundation look like?

Well, to begin with it's not Maybelline. Instead, it'll consist of obtaining a clear, and more accurate picture of your entire financial situation.

Looking at and recording everything you have to your name and breaking down your income in a far more detailed way than you ever have done before.

This will involve getting comfortable looking at your payslip and learning to better understand taxes along with pension contributions.

Once we know what we've got and what we have coming in, we can start investigating what's leaving so that we can better our ability to save.

We will cover where to save, what accounts are best and even what to save for. And finally, we will create a system for you to keep track of and automate all of this. So, whilst your money is working, you can be drinking!

Now, if you're self-employed or run your own business and have read about Lloyd's position and the breaking down of a payslip and are now thinking about how to get your money back, don't worry.

There is still plenty that you can take from this book.

To ensure that you take the necessary steps to reach financial freedom, there will be a to-do list at the end of each chapter called **Your Maze Checklist**.

By completing this, you can be confident that you will have taken all there is from this book and are fully committed to taking control of your finances.

And now it's that time in every introduction where I go on a ten-minute spile about how great I am, how successful I am, and why you must listen to me because I've done this, and I've done that.

No. This isn't that kind of book. I believe that the only metric to which I can prove that this book actually works will be through the results that you achieve.

I'm a fair guy, so if you finish this book, complete each task on your to-do list and honestly feel you are no better off. Then, drop me an email, at:

will@the-money-maze.co.uk

and I'll refund you each and every penny.

Enough chit-chat; let's get into it.

CHAPTER ONE

Where Is My Money?
Assets, Liabilities, & Net Wealth

"If you don't know the problem, you can't have a solution."

While practically everyone agrees with this statement in their heads, our actions might be saying otherwise.

Rather than setting out to have a proper grasp of the financial system (and their financial life), some people believe that someday a multi-billion-dollar idea will pop up in their head. And... they'll wake up to a hundred-thousand pounds lying idle in their bank account and their face plastered on the front cover of Forbes.

Sadly, this doesn't often work that way. As you should know by now, getting wealthy is all about knowledge.

Since this book is in your hands, I can bet that you aren't one of these individuals. Luckily for you, I'm about to take you on a journey that will be a significantly change the way that you lead your life.

In this chapter, we will be looking into the fundamentals of personal finance- assets, liabilities, and net wealth.

Using simple-to-grasp wordings, I'll guide you through the meanings of these terms and then provide a step-by-step outline on how to apply them.

So, let's cut the crap and go straight into it.

Where is your money?

Before we go into the intricate details of measuring your present wealth, let's have a look at where it may be stored. Although money can be stored in many different ways, it is preferably kept in bank accounts.

There are different types of bank accounts- ranging from simple ones such as a basic bank account to more complex ones such as a student bank account.

Let's start by focusing on the most commonly used.

Current Accounts

Current accounts are ingrained into our daily lives, and it's probably the type of account to which you are most familiar, as you'll likely have one if you have a job.

Since we are in the 21st century, there is a good chance your employer doesn't pay your wages in cash; instead, you are paid electronically.

This is possible due to the standardised sort codes and account numbers which enable the easy transfer of money between individuals. Current accounts allow you spend the money you've deposited quickly and simply. Hence, it is safe to say that owning a current account offers convenience to you as a person.

However, this comes at a price that differentiates current accounts from savings accounts.

Savings Accounts

Unlike current accounts, savings accounts allow you to deposit your money while earning a higher rate of interest- depending on the rates that your bank offers.

Interest refers to the amount of money you are paid for lending your money out, in this case, to the bank.

The interest you earn is usually measured in terms of **APR** (Annual Percentage Rate), which is the rate you earn on an account over one year.

For example, if you open a savings account and make an initial deposit of **£10,000** and your bank compounds interest annually with a **0.07% APR,** you will earn about **£7**.

The interest is paid to your account at the end of the year, or sometimes monthly, and your new account balance will begin earning interest.

This is why you should always do your research before opening a savings account.

Now that you have a broad overview of the two main places that you may be keeping your money. Don't get ahead of yourself and judge your entire financial situation on what these accounts might add up to.

Although this might seem like a great way to measure your wealth, please don't use this method.

Why?

Because wealth isn't as simple as a measure of the things that you own- the things that you owe also need to be taken into consideration.

You might even have other forms of wealth, which aren't shown as numbers on your online banking app.

Assets

To begin with, think about this question: What do you think an asset is, and what assets do you think that you own?

Take a piece of paper and write your answer down.

Done?

Really done?

Okay...here's what I'd call an asset: An asset is anything- and I mean anything- of monetary value.

Hence, the **£10** note in your wallet, the large following on your Instagram page and your most cherished mobile phone are all assets.

Assets can be classified based on physical presence or their ease of convertibility to cash.

On the basis of a physical presence, assets can be classified into two broad groups: **Tangible** and **intangible** assets.

As the name implies, **intangible** assets include resources without a physical presence, such as patents, copyrights, and leases.

Whilst tangible assets refer to assets that have a physical presence, including properties and financial investments.

Liquid Assets

Liquid assets can be converted into cash very quickly.

They can also be referred to as current assets, as they can be sold or traded with minimal impact on their value.

A prime example of a liquid asset is cash itself because, well, it's cash. Other examples of liquid assets include money market assets and mutual funds- basically anything you own that can be exchanged for money within the blink of an eye.

This all depends on having many available buyers at any one time however.

For instance, take a look at the financial market; selling stocks is as easy as hitting "sell" on your iPhone.

This is because of the overwhelming amount of people and organisations interested in purchasing these stocks, just as you are about to sell them.

Non-liquid Assets

Unlike liquid assets, non-liquid assets are not readily convertible to cash. Usually, these kinds of assets are intended for long-term possession. An example of a this is property.

The ease of selling a house can't be compared to the simplicity of selling a stock; it might take months to find a buyer and then another few months for it to actually go through.

Hence, although non-liquid assets can have a significant monetary value, you cannot really depend on them for your immediate spending needs.

What are your assets?

Now that we understand what an asset is, let's get more practical.

A great way to record all your assets is on a spreadsheet.

I know that creating a spreadsheet that does everything you want is no easy job. Asides from being tedious, it's very time-consuming.

So, to make sure that you spend all your energy taking the steps in this book, rather than trying to figure out how excel works, I have created one for you.

I've even done this using Google Sheets, which is still accessible without the Microsoft Office Suite.

To get access to this spreadsheet, simply scan the Q.R. code below, or visit: **www.the-money-maze.co.uk**

This particular spreadsheet will be referenced throughout our examples, as it's the one that our mate Lloyd will be using in his demonstrations.

This way, following along for the majority of you will be a whole lot easier.

If you do want to go ahead and make your own, that's totally fine! (Bet it won't be as good, though).

Right, now that's been established, let's head back to business.

Knowing what an asset is, isn't enough; we know how and where to record them.

Let's have a look at Lloyd's assets:

Assets	Value	Liabilities	Value
Barclay's Current Account	£350.00		
Barclay's Savings Account	£50.00		
Vauxhall Corsa	£4,000.00		
Total Assets	**£4,400.00**	**Total Liabilities**	**£0.00**

He currently has **£350** in his current account, **£50** in his savings account, and a car currently worth **£4,000** in the market.

By adding these to his spreadsheet, we can see his assets add up to **£4,400.**

In all likelihood, you'll have a more extensive list of assets than Lloyd (and that's perfectly cool).

How far should you go with this then? Well, don't start recording the pencils in your desk drawer as a monterey asset.

They technically could be, but you'll never stop if you go down this path!

To start off with, try recording anything you own worth over **£500.00**, plus any bank balances you have, on the **Initial Wealth Tab** of your spreadsheet, under **Assets**.

While recording your assets, you should keep in mind that not everything you own will be the worth as much as you brought it for.

This is due to a concept people in the business world call **depreciation**.

Depreciation refers to the gradual decline in the value of an asset over time, either due to wear and tear or fluctuations in the market.

In personal finance, items such as appliances and cars tend to fall into this category.

An excellent way to find out the present value of your depreciating assets- for instance, your car- is to explore the internet to see the price people pay for said items today.

Although there might be varying prices, this gives you a rough idea of how much they're worth.

Your Goal in the Game

As a financially savvy person looking to build wealth, your goal should be to acquire assets to generate an income- hence, the assets you acquire should make your pockets heavier than, you know, less heavy.

When you do this, the business gurus might say you are engaged in a concept known as an **investment**.

In simple terms, an **investment** refers to an asset you've obtained with the goal of it **appreciating** (to go up in value).

To invest, you need to let go of some sort of capital- whether it be your time, money, or effort- to acquire an asset that will make you a profit.

Liabilities

While looking at your assets might create a picture of your financial standing, balancing what you own against what you owe is what puts the icing on the cake.

In other words, you should put conscious effort into analysing the things you've borrowed in the past.

As you will come to know, debts and loans can be used synonymously; however, loans tend to be more specific kinds of debts.

The term **debt** refers to something—anything— borrowed by one person from another.

Whilst **loans** refer to an agreement between two parties in which one party lends money to another, which will be repaid, alongside interest.

Many people acquire debts and loans to purchase a service or commodity that they wouldn't be able to otherwise afford, and so the the interest rates that are set can significantly impact the amount of money repaid to the lender.

What are interest rates?

Interest Rates in this context simply refer to the amount of money—usually expressed in an **Annual Percentage Rate** (APR)—which a lender charges on the amount loaned out.

Hence, it is the sum of money paid by the debtor for the privilege of borrowing money—asides from the original amount.

So, let's say that you borrow **£1,000** at a **3%** APR, you'd then have to repay **£1,030**.

Good Debts vs Bad Debts

Good debts are those that when obtained, are used to purchase assets that will increase in value. From our previous definition of investments, it is safe to say that good debt is obtained for investment purposes.

If the debt helps you purchase items that will help you build your income or add to your net worth (which we will come to later), then it is classed as good debt.

The three main types of good debts include: student loans—which are used for educational purposes; business loans—which are used for company expansion or establishment; and mortgages—which are used to help purchase property or land.

Debt can also be classified as **bad debt** when it is used to purchase a depreciating asset.

Any asset that will decrease—rather than increase in value—is termed a **depreciating asset**.

This includes clothes, electronics, and most cars, which unfortunately aren't the best uses of our money, especially if it's not ours.

How do I record my debts?

Let's hop back to our spreadsheet, namely the **Liabilities Column**.

Liabilities simply refer to each debt a person or company has.

From a personal finance perspective, liabilities can include any credit cards, car loans, and other various types of buy now, pay later schemes.

Before we get our hands dirty however, let's take a look at Lloyd's liabilities:

Assets	Value	Liabilities	Value
Barclay's Current Account	£350.00	Sainsbury's Credit Card	£700.00
Barclay's Savings Account	£50.00	HSBC Credit Card	£3,000.00
Vauxhall Corsa	£4,000.00	Car Finance	£4,500.00
Total Assets	**£4,400.00**	**Total Liabilities**	**£8,200.00**

Lloyd has two credit cards: a **Sainsbury's Credit Card** which he owes **£700**, and a **HSBC Credit Card** to which he owes **£3,000**, along with a **Car Finance** worth **£4,500**, meaning that his total liabilities add up to **£8,200**.

You will notice that most of Lloyd's debts are bad debts. That is, these liabilities aren't a current or potential source of income for Lloyd.

For instance, look at the car finance loan Lloyd has taken out.

As previously mentioned, a car can be a depreciating asset. So, immediately after Lloyd got the keys, hopped into his new car, and drove off to meet his girlfriend, the car's market value immediately decreased.

Since the car's new market value is below Lloyd's outstanding balance on the car loan, Lloyd can be said to have a negative equity on the car.

Generally, **negative equity** is a term used to describe owing more on an item than that item is actually worth.

As a rule of thumb, you shouldn't go into debt over any item that could be a source of negative equity in the future, although it is always a risk.

Once you've recorded your liabilities down too, it's time to work out your net wealth.

What's your net wealth?

In all likelihood, you know the net worth of the famous business moguls. You've seen the word plastered everywhere- but do you know what yours is?

Net wealth is used to determine an individual's overall financial position, and so being able to calculate this yourself is a great place to start.

Ready?

Okay! Let's head back to Lloyd to find out his net wealth; that way, you can do the same.

Put in mind that the net wealth- or net worth- of an individual is simply the value of their assets owned minus their liabilities.

Net worth = *(Total value of Assets) – (Total value of liabilities)*

In Lloyd's case, that's:

£4,400 - £8,200 = -£3,800.

And unfortunately for him, it's negative.

On the other hand, if the value of Lloyd's assets exceeds that of his liabilities, then Lloyd would have a positive net worth.

Poor Lloyd! Well, at least he didn't actually have to do this maths himself as it was all done for him, thanks to his lovely spreadsheet.

Total Assets	£4,400.00	Total Liabilities	£8,200.00
	Net Wealth	-£3,800.00	

As we can see, your financial position is more than just the digits on your mobile banking app, and financial intelligence goes further than just scribbling your down your income.

The most important thing is that understanding this helps you form a clear picture of where you are headed.

I'll take you deeper into the financial world as you read on, simplifying over-your-head business lingo using easy-to-understand everyday terms.

Your ideologies about certain concepts will be corrected, which will spur you to take painful- although helpful- financial decisions.

As Jim Rohn puts it: *"We must all suffer from one of two pains: the pain of discipline or the pain of regret. The difference is that discipline weighs ounces whilst regret weighs tons."*

So, choose: the pain of financial discipline or the pain of regret?

Your Maze Checklist:

Before moving on to the next chapter, complete the following tasks, if you haven't already:

1. Record both your **Assets & Liabilities** on the **Initial Wealth Tab** of your spreadsheet.

If you have a student loan, however, don't both inputting it; I'll explain why later.

There is also no need to use the £ symbols, or minus signs when recording your information, as this it has been configured to do this automatically.

2. Calculate your **Net Wealth**. (Which should have been already done for you).

CHAPTER TWO

Where Else Is My Money Kept?
Let's Talk Payslips & Pensions

What if I told you that you had money in some places, places that you do not even know existed?

The truth is, not everyone knows where all their money is being kept. So as these words breeze past your eyes, you may have some money hiding in secret locations.

If this excites you, you should read on because I promise to be an undercover spy in this chapter.

I will take the veil off your eyes and help you see clearly what most people don't. And then, with the information available to you, you will be able to make much better financial decisions.

Now, for those of you who are self-employed this bit might not be so relevant to you. However, it is still worth a read as you might still learn a few things, which may be useful if you are considering hiring staff.

As for anyone who is slave to a boss, let me ask you.

When did you last study your payslip?

Of a truth, your payslip will give you the best idea of your actual income and so it is important that you gain an understanding of all its jargon.

An Overview of Payslips

In the UK, every employee is entitled to a written payslip issued before or during payment.

This written payslip doesn't have to be on paper- it could either be sent to you by email or viewed via an online portal.

Although payslips differ from one another, the majority of information found is usually the same.

Not everyone receives a payslip- for instance, freelancers.

However, if you do receive a payslip.

You must keep it.

And I'll give you two reasons why I recommend that you do so:

Firstly, payslips contain a lot of information about you and what you earn. A glance at your payslip can reveal many intricate details not everyone should know- such as your National Insurance number.

Secondly, to obtain most financial products- such as loans- you might be asked to present proof of pay, by showing your last three payslips.

Hence, for recordkeeping purposes, safeguard your payslip.

Deconstructing your Payslip

Understanding your payslip can be quite simple.

So, why not give me a chance to prove that to you?

Let's begin with your **base pay**. As the name suggests, your base pay is the initial salary paid to an employee, excluding any benefits, bonuses, and or overtime. (It may also be referred to as your **pensionable pay**).

An individual's annual salary is calculated by multiplying their base pay by the number of times that they are paid.

Let's look at Lloyd's payslip and see what we can find there.

Payslip

Pay Date	: 2022/06/30	Employee ID	: 123456789
Pay Period	: 2022/06/01 - 2022/06/30	Employee Name	: Lloyd Maze

Earnings	Amount	Deductions	Amount
Base Pay	1693.55	Tax	112.28
Gross Pay	1608.88	NI Contribution	74.38
		Pension Contribution	84.67
		Workers Union	8.74
Total Earnings	1693.55	Total Deductions	280.07
		Net Pay	1413.48

1413.48
One Thousand Four Hundred Thirteen And Forty Eight

Lloyd here has a base pay of **£1,693.55**. Also known in the business world as "almost two fat ones!!"

To calculate Lloyd's annual salary, we will need to multiply his base pay by 12 (how often he gets paid).

Giving Lloyd a yearly salary roughly of **£20,322.60**.

Pensions

Let's go over the basics:

If you work in the UK as an employee, then there are few ways in which you might build a pension. But first, what is a pension?

Well, your pension is a gift to your future self, as it helps you create a source of income after retirement.

These include state pensions, workplace pensions and personal pensions.

If you're self-employed however, you'll have to go about setting one up yourself. This will be covered in some additional content that I am creating for my website, to which you will have free access once released.

Workplace Pensions

These kinds of pensions are usually arranged by employers for their employees.

As a worker who is at least 22, earning **£10,000** a year or over, you'll be automatically enrolled into a workplace pension scheme.

As you might guess, this is known as **automatic enrolment**.

There are two different types of workplace pensions:

A **defined benefit pension scheme** provides a guaranteed pension income when you retire.

However, what you will earn is dependent on the salary you've earned during service and the length of years you've been part of the scheme.

For example, if you work in the public sector or for a large employer, you might be on this type of workplace pension.

Defined benefit schemes have a retirement age that is usually around age **65**- at which you are entitled to your pension benefits.

However, the rules can differ across some schemes.

A **defined contribution pension scheme** instead, involves building up a pot that will pay you a retirement income.

Unlike a defined benefit pension scheme that promises a definite income after retirement, how much you'll get is determined by how much you contributed and how that money has been invested to grow.

So, you might be tempted to ask- what determines my levels of contribution?

Easy: You and your employer.

If we have another look at Lloyd's payslip, we can see that he is paying in (contributing) **£84.67** towards his pension each month.

Payslip

Pay Date	: 2022/06/30	Employee ID	: 123456789
Pay Period	: 2022/06/01 - 2022/06/30	Employee Name	: Lloyd Maze

Earnings	Amount	Deductions	Amount
Base Pay	1693.55	Tax	112.28
Gross Pay	1608.88	NI Contribution	74.38
		Pension Contribution	84.67
		Workers Union	8.74
Total Earnings	1693.55	Total Deductions	280.07
		Net Pay	1413.48

1413.48
One Thousand Four Hundred Thirteen And Forty Eight

How do I join a workplace pension scheme?

Your employer.

As long as you meet the earlier criteria (aged **22** and over, earn at least **£10,000** a year), you are automatically enrolled into a pension scheme.

Usually, your employer will have sent you a written letter about this pension scheme, which tends to include:

- The date you were added.
- The type of pension scheme that it is.
- How much they will contribute and how much you need to contribute as well.
- How to leave if you wish (you've still got freewill).
- Along with how tax relief applies to you.

If keeping track of important documents isn't your strong suit, then now is the time to start. Luckily, if you've lost track of your pension details, Pension tracing services can help you find the information you need. Simply visit:

https://www.gov.uk/find-pension-contact-details

Or speak with someone at work.

Note- Your employer is not obliged to automatically enrol you if you've been issued a notice that you'll be leaving your job. Or if you've given notice that you'll be leaving.

Also remember that employer cannot force you to opt out of a workplace pension or unfairly discriminate against you for being in one.

How do I view and access my pension pot?

Managing your pension pot is no big deal. In fact, with the correct details, you can access it in a few clicks.

In all likelihood, your pension scheme provider will have a website through which you can access your records.

If your pension scheme provider is somehow stuck in the Stone Age and lacks a website, they will instead send you a letter annually with your current pot's value.

If you have trouble finding a recent copy, your best bet will be to get in touch with them- asking them to resend it to you.

Note- Some pension scheme providers have offers and links littered all over their websites. So, for now, when you go looking on their website, stick to your goal: view your pot's current value, get your bags, and run.

How much does my employer contribute?

The amount you- and your employer- pay towards your pension depends on two main factors: the type of workplace pension scheme you are enrolled in and whether you were automatically enrolled or opted in voluntarily.

You are also able to get tax relief on your pension contributions as this is the government's way of helping you retire.

For people who have been automatically enrolled, both you and your employer will contribute a certain percentage of your earnings into your pension.

Your employer's contribution will be outside of your usual salary, and so is extra income that you are receiving!

From April 2019, a new law ensures that the minimum your employer pays in is **3%** of your base salary.

However, this new law also states that the total minimum contribution to your workplace pension needs to be **8%**.

Hence, you'll need to settle the balance- **5%** which will come from your pocket.

As we discovered earlier, Lloyd is paying **£84.67** into his pension scheme- which amounts to **5%** of his base salary of **£1,693.55**.

What's not recorded on his payslip, however, are the contributions that his employer is also making. (The extra **3%** that we were talking about).

This is what I mean by having money in secret places. Lloyd could be earning an extra **3%** on top of his annual salary, if not more, that he didn't even know about because one, it's not recorded on his payslip, and two, it doesn't go into his bank account each month.

And if you're anything like Lloyd, then you'll be getting extra money too.

In some cases, employers actually choose to pay in more than is legally obliged. In this case, you could really be quid's in.

This is as close to free money as you can get, so understanding how to use this to your advantage is vital.

For example, your employer might only pay in more if you do so (they'll match your contributions), and so by upping your contribution an extra **5%**, you may be able to in turn increase your earnings by an additional **5%** too.

On the other side of the river, if you weren't automatically enrolled but opted in voluntarily, your employer is not legally entitled to contribute the legal minimum amount if you earn less than **£520** a month, **£120** a week or **£480** over **4** weeks.

What if I've worked for more than one employer?

This chapter is all about finding our hidden treasures (in this case, pension pots). Well, if you've worked for more than one employer in the past, you might have an island full of them.

I'm sure you get the point I'm trying to make. Since you may have worked for many employers, your pension pot will be split into separate schemes. So, the question is: how do you find how much you've got?

Easy: By using the same tool we did earlier to find our missing pension details:

www.gov.uk/find-pension-contact-details

Note- this service only gives you the information about your previous employers' pension scheme providers, not intricate details, like say how much is in it.

You'll then have to reach out to that pension scheme provider, asking whether you have a pension with them and, if so, how rich you are.

Why is learning about pensions and payslips important?

Pensions and payslips are not taught in schools. But nevertheless, hopefully you've now got a pretty decent idea of what they are.

An understanding of payslips and pensions gives us a better insight into where our money is. Hence, we, (including our mate Lloyd) can now view our financial situation in an entirely new light.

Your Maze Checklist:

Since the basics about payslips and pensions are now clear to you, you must (yeah, must) complete the following tasks before moving on to the next chapter.

1. First off, I need you to dust off your documents and look for your most recent payslip.

2. From your payslip, work out your **base pay**.

3. Then calculate your annual salary.

4. Go to your HR department or boss and get all the available information about the pension scheme that you are currently enrolled in.

5. From the information obtained, work out if you are contributing to the pension. If so, how much?

6. Then workout how much your employer contributes (this will usually be a percentage and not an exact figure).

7. Log in to your provider's website and access your pension pot.

How much do you currently have hiding away?

8. If you've worked for more than one employer in the past, find the pension details of these employers using the approved government site mentioned here:

www.gov.uk/find-pension-contact-details

9. Finally, add these accounts again to the **Initial Wealth Tab** of your spreadsheet, giving you a complete overview of your finances.

10. Re-calculate your new **Net Wealth**. Bit better right?

CHAPTER THREE

Where Does My Money Go?
Taxes & Other Deductions

During the previous chapter, I'd like to think that calculated your annual salary.

I'm guessing you'd probably beat your chest, saying that can't be what I earn. If so, how do I end up with so little?

One possible explanation is that somehow, your quid's got wings (which, unfortunately, is not true).

Okay, enough jokes for now. But really, why do you seem to earn so much and yet get paid so little?

The answer is simple: taxes. You see, before you even handle the cash you are paid each month, a certain amount of money is deducted from your earnings.

And most of these deductions are in the form of taxes.

So, what the hell are taxes?

To begin with, taxes are not penalties. Neither are they fines.

Taxes are simply deductions or financial charges placed by the government on something you own (such as your income) or something you buy (such as goods and services).

The aim of collecting these taxes is to build a public pot of money that the government can then use to finance societal projects- including infrastructure and law enforcement.

With the aid of taxes, the government can improve the standard of living for UK citizens, things from emergency services to very basics amenities such as good roads and streetlights. (Although if you've driven in the UK, which I'm sure that you have, you probably won't believe me).

The UK has, in my opinion, has too many taxes.

These taxes can be **direct** while others are **indirect**.

Direct taxes are usually placed on the profit or the income an individual earns.

Whilst **indirect taxes** are taxes placed on goods and services purchased by an individual rather than that individual's income.

An example of an indirect tax is **Value Added Tax (VAT)**.

These taxes are less evident because they are integrated into the prices of the items you purchase- rather than a direct deduction from your income.

Asides from these two types of taxes, there are other kinds of UK tax, which I'll list below:

- Corporation tax
- Council tax
- Capital gains tax
- Inheritance tax

...and a thousand more types of tax which really don't concern you. Instead of offloading what every kind of tax in the UK entails, I'll rather focus on the one that hit you hardest every month:

Income taxes.

Just as the name implies, **income tax** is a tax you pay on what you earn.

Before the money hits your bank account, income taxes are usually deducted from your **gross pay**.

Gross pay refers to the total amount earned, including overtime and bonuses, minus your pension contributions.

So how does your employer (or pension provider) know how much you remove from your salary?

Simple: Tax codes.

Tax Codes- A Brief Overview

Tax codes refer to a combination of a few numbers and a letter given to you to show the **HMRC** (Her Majesty's Revenue & Customs) how much tax you should be paying.

The amount of tax you pay depends on how much income you have, your personal allowance and how much tax you've already paid in that year.

As previously mentioned, your tax code will contain several numbers and a letter. For most people who have one job or pension, for instance, Lloyd (who's loyal to just one boss) has the tax code **1257L**.

So, what does this mean?

Let's begin with the numbers: Your tax code numbers simply dictate to your employer how much tax-free income you get in each **tax year**, which runs from the 6th of April to the 5th of April.

This tax-free income is known as your **personal allowance** and currently, the standard going rate for the 2022/23 tax year is **£12,570**.

This means you can earn up to **£12,570** without paying any income tax; the amount earned above this threshold however will then incur a tax at a tax rate.

Here's where most people get it mixed up, so pay attention:

Tax bracket one (**the basic rate**) consists of individuals who earn between **£12,571** and **£50,270**.

These people will pay a tax rate of **20%** on anything over their personal allowance.

Tax bracket two (**the higher rate**) consists of those who earn between **£50,271- £150,000**.

These lucky individuals will still pay **20%** tax on anything between **£12,571** and **£50,270** and then **40%** on earnings over **£50,271**.

This continues up to tax bracket three (**the additional rate**).

Again, using the same system, they'll pay **20%** on their first **£12,571** to **£50,270**, **40%** on earnings between **£50,271** and **£150,000** and then a whopping **45%** on anything over **£150,001**.

With that said, let's bring Lloyd back in to help clarify things a little more for us.

Since most of the people reading this book will fall into tax bracket one- that is, I'm assuming buying a beginner's personal finance book means you earn between **£12,571- £50,270** – let's assume Lloyd does too.

That said, Lloyd's **base pay** is **£1,693.55** per month. However, he doesn't pay tax on this amount.

Instead, he will have to pay tax on his **gross pay/taxable income**.

This happens to be **£1,608.88**, as this is what's remaining after he's paid into his pension.

In a year, Lloyd is paid 12 times. Hence, his gross pay needs to be multiplied by 12.

£1,608.88 × 12 = £19,306.56

This is his taxable income for the entire tax year.

However, remember that we all get a personal allowance, right?

To determine how much tax Lloyd actually has to pay, we need to subtract his personal allowance from his taxable income for the year.

£19,306.56 - £12,570 = £6,736.56

This means that Lloyd only pays **20%** on **£6,736.56**, not **£19,306.56**.

20% of £6,736.56 = £1,347.31

As we can see, that's an awful lot of tax, and so rather than him being charged in one big hit, this amount is also divided by the number of times he gets paid (12), leaving him with a tax payment of **£112.28**.

£1,347.31 ÷ 12 = £112.28

Payslip

Pay Date   : 2022/06/30   Employee ID   : 123456789
Pay Period   : 2022/06/01 - 2022/06/30 Employee Name   : Lloyd Maze

Earnings	Amount	Deductions	Amount
Base Pay	1693.55	Tax	112.28
Gross Pay	1608.88	NI Contribution	74.38
		Pension Contribution	84.67
		Workers Union	8.74
Total Earnings	1693.55	Total Deductions	280.07
		Net Pay	1413.48

1413.48
One Thousand Four Hundred Thirteen And Forty Eight

While the above tax rates hold true in most parts of the UK, the tax game in Scotland is a little different.

Although the personal allowance is the same, if you call Scotland your home, then you'll pay these rates instead:

- Starter rate: **£12,571.00 - £14,667.00 – 19%**

- Basic rate: **£14,668.00 - £25,296.00 – 20%**

- Intermediate rate: **£25,297.00 - £43,662.00 – 21%**

- Higher rate: **£43,663 - £150,000 – 41%**

- Top rate: Over **£150,000 - 46%**

If this isn't enough detail for you, then to find out more about paying tax in Scotland, you can visit:

https://www.gov.uk/scottish-income-tax

Now that you have a firm grip over the meaning of the numbers found on tax codes let's briefly look at what the letters mean:

L: You are entitled to the standard personal allowance for that tax year and will be charged based on this.

M: You've received **10%** of your partner's personal allowance- if you are currently on marriage allowance.

N: You've transferred **10%** of your personal allowance to your partner.

OT: When you begin a new job, and your employer does not have the details they need, you are placed on this code.

NT: You are not being taxed on your income.

C: Your tax rate is based on rates in Wales.

S: Your tax rate is based on rates in Scotland.

WI, MI, X: You've been placed on an emergency tax code.

What are emergency tax codes?

These are temporary tax codes that you are put on if HMRC doesn't have the correct details about your income.

Usually, this occurs after a change in circumstances, such as getting a new job or switching to be an employee after being self-employed.

If you overpay tax during the period that you have an emergency tax code, you'll be entitled to getting this money back.

Another deduction: National insurance contributions

National insurance contributions are a fee you've got to pay to build up your entitlement to certain benefits such as maternity allowance and the state pension.

Unless you have a sufficient national insurance contribution, you might not be able to access some of these benefits.

In the UK, you are mandated to pay national insurance if you are **16** and over, and:

You are an employee who earns at least **£190** a week (soon to be **£242**, as of July 2022).

Before you begin paying national insurance however, you are issued a national insurance number.

Your **national insurance number** consists of letters and numbers- and unlike your tax code- it never changes!

The main factors that affect what you pay are your employment status and how much you earn.

National insurance contributions are grouped in classes based on these factors.

If you are employed, you will pay the **Class 1 national insurance rate**.

You'll pay **13.25%** of your yearly earnings from **£12,570** to **£50,270**, and then **3.25%** of your earnings above **£50,270**.

As Lloyd is employed-he falls under this class.

Therefore, just like a tax, national insurance is charged on Lloyd's gross/taxable income- which, in this case, is **£19,306.56**.

He'll pay **13.25%** on **£6,736.56**, as that's the amount he earns over the **£12,750** threshold.

£19,306.56 - £12,750 = £6,736.56

13.25% of £6,736.56 = £892.59

£892.59 ÷ 12 =£74.38

Payslip

Pay Date	: 2022/06/30	Employee ID	: 123456789
Pay Period	: 2022/06/01 - 2022/06/30	Employee Name	: Lloyd Maze

Earnings	Amount	Deductions	Amount
Base Pay	1693.55	Tax	112.28
Gross Pay	1608.88	NI Contribution	74.38
		Pension Contribution	84.67
		Workers Union	8.74
Total Earnings	1693.55	Total Deductions	280.07
		Net Pay	1413.48

1413.48
One Thousand Four Hundred Thirteen And Forty Eight

As I previously mentioned, your national insurance contributions allow you to access some nice little benefits, including the state pension.

The state pension is a regular payment you can receive from the government once you reach a certain age, referred to as your **state pension age**.

If you are a man born before 6th of April 1951 or a woman born before 6th of April 1953, you are eligible for the **basic state pension**- which is currently tagged at **£141.85** per week.

You most likely do not fall into this category if you are reading this book. However, as a man born after the 6th of April 1951 and a woman born after the 6th of April 1953, you are eligible for the **new state pension**.

For the 2022/23 tax year, the state pension is currently worth **£185.15** per week, which amounts to **£9,627.80** annually.

However, if you have gaps in your national insurance records, it might be lower.

To receive the bare minimum, you need to have at least 10 years of national insurance contributions and will need **35** qualifying years to get the full cake.

So, what is a qualifying year? Basically, a year can be tagged as 'qualifying' if:

• You're employed (to a single employer) and earn more than **£242** a week, therefore paying your national insurance contributions.

• You're employed (to a single employer) but earn between **£123** and **£242** a week, you'll be treated as having paid your contributions (to protect your record).

• You receive National insurance credits.

• You constantly make voluntary National insurance contributions.

If there are periods in your career where you couldn't pay your national insurance for one reason or another, don't fret- you might be able to claim national insurance credits.

You are qualified for this if:

- You are unemployed or earn a low-income.

- You haven't been at work due to an illness.

- You are completing jury service.

- You are disabled.

- You are on paternity or maternity leave.

Gaps may be present within your records if you've been self-employed or worked from abroad during your career.

In this case, there is an option to make voluntary contributions- also known as **Class 3 contributions**- to fill in those gaps.

Although you'll then miss out of some of the other benefits you might want to take advantage of in the future, such as Jobseeker's Allowance.

What about these other deductions on my payslip?

While I've now covered the major deductions you'd encounter - tax and national contributions - you might still find other deductions on your payslip.

For instance, pension schemes.

Yes, Will, I already know about pension schemes; you wouldn't shut up about them earlier.

However, whilst this statement may be true, there are still some bits I missed. And so, I'd love to reiterate my point.

If you remember from earlier, employers tend to automatically deduct our pension contribution from our base pay, rather than our gross pay, serving as a form of **automatic tax relief**.

If you notice that your pension doesn't appear to be set on this kind of relief, don't worry too much.

Your income should instead be taxed as usual, and then your pension provider will claim tax relief on your contributions and then add the difference to your pension pot.

This is known as **relief at source**.

With the information gathered earlier in this book, you should be able to figure out what kind of tax relief your pension attracts.

Any issues, drop me an email.

Moving on, you may still have some other not-so-tax friendly deductions leaving your payslip.

Deductions such as parking permits, union fees and student loans need to also be considered.

Payslip

| Pay Date | : 2022/06/30 | Employee ID | : 123456789 |
| Pay Period | : 2022/06/01 - 2022/06/30 | Employee Name | : Lloyd Maze |

Earnings	Amount	Deductions	Amount
Base Pay	1693.55	Tax	112.28
Gross Pay	1608.88	NI Contribution	74.38
		Pension Contribution	84.67
		Workers Union	8.74
Total Earnings	1693.55	Total Deductions	280.07
		Net Pay	1413.48

1413.48
One Thousand Four Hundred Thirteen And Forty Eight

After all of these deductions, whatever is left will be your **net pay**.

Payslip

| Pay Date | : 2022/06/30 | Employee ID | : 123456789 |
| Pay Period | : 2022/06/01 - 2022/06/30 | Employee Name | : Lloyd Maze |

Earnings	Amount	Deductions	Amount
Base Pay	1693.55	Tax	112.28
Gross Pay	1608.88	NI Contribution	74.38
		Pension Contribution	84.67
		Workers Union	8.74
Total Earnings	1693.55	Total Deductions	280.07
		Net Pay	1413.48

1413.48
One Thousand Four Hundred Thirteen And Forty Eight

While many people may assume that this is what they are being paid per month, you now know otherwise, and so does our good friend Lloyd.

Your Maze Checklist:

Here's what you've got to do before moving on to the next chapter:

1. Get your payslip out for some analysis. Work out:

   What you are paying in taxes.

   What you're paying in national insurance.

   And what other deductions might be leaving your payslip.

2. Look for any discrepancies and if found contact HMRC to resolve them.

3. Check your national insurance record by creating a government ID (if you don't have one already), then take notes of any gaps.

This can be done by heading to:

https://www.gov.uk/check-national-insurance-record

CHAPTER FOUR

What Should I Do Next?
Recording Expenses & Cutting Bills

After reading the last chapter, I bet you now know more about pensions and taxes than you have done before. If you already knew about all this, then, it's time to get practical.

You've been given quite a bit of homework so far, so let's use all that hard work to sort out our spreadsheet.

Begin by opening the **Monthly Expenses Tab**.

When you do, you will be greeted by three columns:

An **Income Column**, a **Monthly Expense Column**, and **Monthly Savings** & **Investment Column**.

Before going on, you should know that I will be using some key terms to describe your personal finances.

First, **pre-tax**, which refers to your income before your tax is calculated.

This includes absolutely everything that you earn, including both your monthly salary and your employer's pension contribution.

Secondly, **pre-pay**, which refers to anything that takes place on your gross/taxable pay, but before the money hits your account.

In other words, this is your income just before you are paid.

These deductions will be referred to as your **pre-pay expenses**, and will include deductions such as your tax, national insurance contribution, and workers' union fees, amongst others.

Clear?

Okay, let's get your finances sorted out.

Begin by inputting your monthly income. Note that this should be calculated based on the bare minimum that you are expecting to receive.

This means you should not include any regular bonuses or overtime just yet. Reason being, what if you do not get these additions?

Your financial budget may come falling down like a pack of stacked cards. Then, of course, you can eventually factor in any extra cash you receive after you've created a budget that can exist without it.

Now, if you happen to have additional pay on your payslip, such as overtime or bonuses, you're going to have record your finances using a mix of both payslip and this salary calculator:

https://www.thesalarycalculator.co.uk/salary.php

Whack in your annual salary and student loan repayment plan, then use the breakdown figures of your base pay (listed as your gross pay on this calculator however), tax, national insurance contributions and student loan payments that this gives you.

Then, use your payslip to record the rest of the information required.

Slightly more complicated I know, and so any issues drop me an email and I'll help to get you sorted.

While recording your monthly salary in the **Income Column**, it is best you begin with your **base pay**, and not your gross or net pay, then slot in your **employer's pension contribution** (as this is money that you are earning too).

If you only know the percentage that your employer contributes, and not the exact amount. Try looking for the exact figure on your online pension portal, as it will not be referenced on your payslip.

If you've been unable to find anything, use this percentage calculator:

https://percentagecalculator.net/

Input the percentage that your employer contributes, followed by your monthly base pay.

This will tell you how much they are contributing, and you can then input that figure into your spreadsheet.

Finally, if you have a second job or side hustle that serves as a regular source of income, input that too.

Since these are all pre-tax values, they should be recorded in the **Green Section**, just here.

Income	Amount	Monthly Expenses	Amount	Monthly Savings & Investments	Amount
Monthly Salary (Base Pay)	£1,693.55				
Employer's Pension Contribution	£169.34				
Total Income (Pre-Tax)	£1,862.89	Total Expenses (Pre-Tax)	£0.00	Total Savings/Investments (Pre-Tax)	£0.00
Total Income (Pre-Pay)	£1,862.89	Total Expenses (Pre-Pay)	£0.00	Total Savings/Investments (Pre-Pay)	£0.00
Total Income (Paid)	£1,862.89	Total Expenses (Paid)	£0.00	Total Savings/Investments (Paid)	£0.00

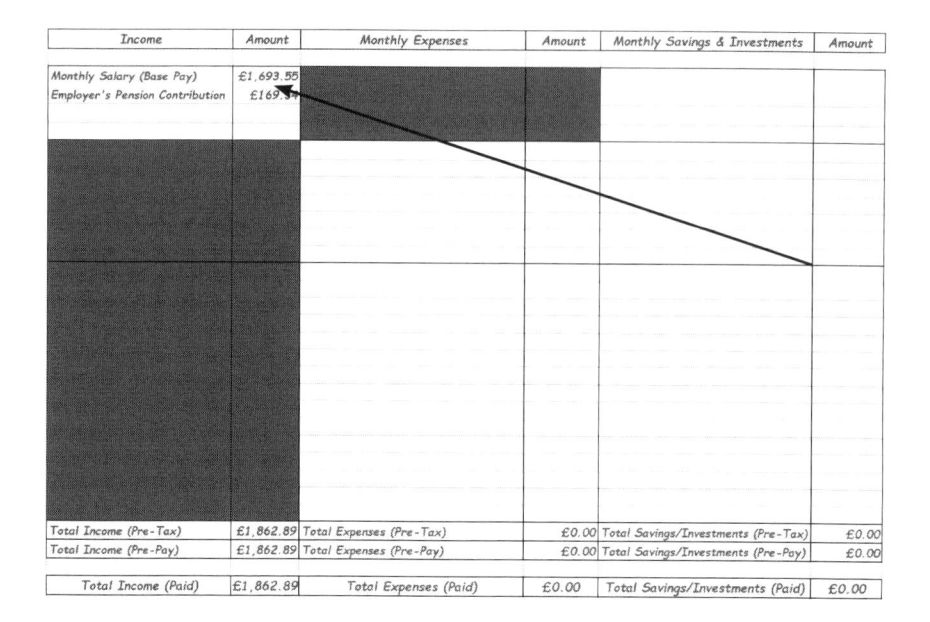

Note: throughout the printed version of this book, the images will be in black and white. So, please refer to the actual spreadsheet if unsure.

Done?

Cool, now head over to the **Monthly Savings & Investment Column**.

Here, list your **personal pension contribution** (found on your payslip) and your **employer's pension contribution** (which we have just worked out).

Again, these should be recorded in the **Green Section** of the spreadsheet, as this all occurs before you are taxed.

Income	Amount	Monthly Expenses	Amount	Monthly Savings & Investments	Amount
Monthly Salary (Base Pay)	£1,693.55			My Pension Contribution	£84.67
Employer's Pension Contribution	£169.34			Employer's Pension Contribution	£169.34
Total Income (Pre-Tax)	£1,862.89	Total Expenses (Pre-Tax)	£0.00	Total Savings/Investments (Pre-Tax)	£254.01
Total Income (Pre-Pay)	£1,608.88	Total Expenses (Pre-Pay)	£0.00	Total Savings/Investments (Pre-Pay)	£0.00
Total Income (Paid)	£1,608.88	Total Expenses (Paid)	£0.00	Total Savings/Investments (Paid)	£0.00

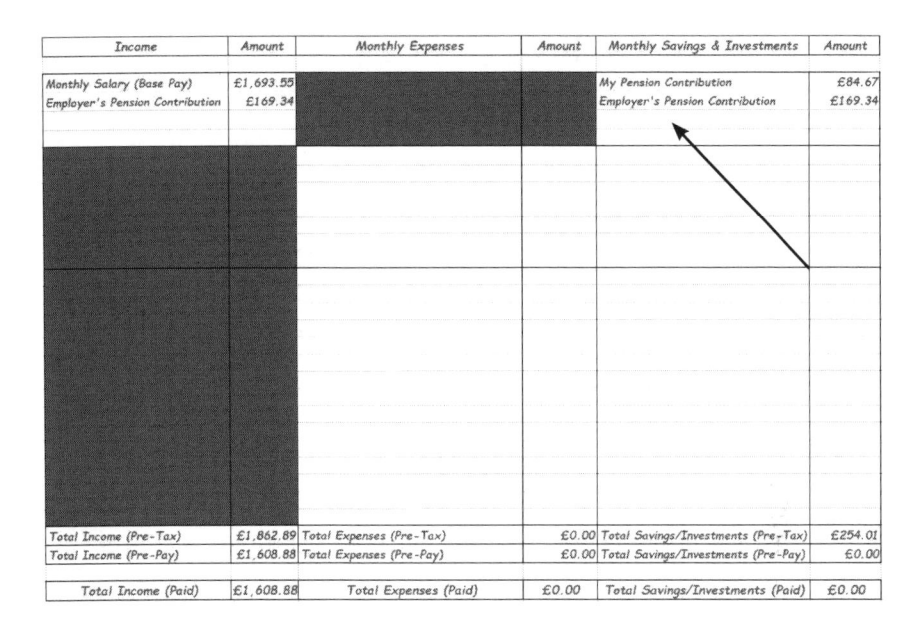

Let's look at what Lloyd's done to better understand what I've just described.

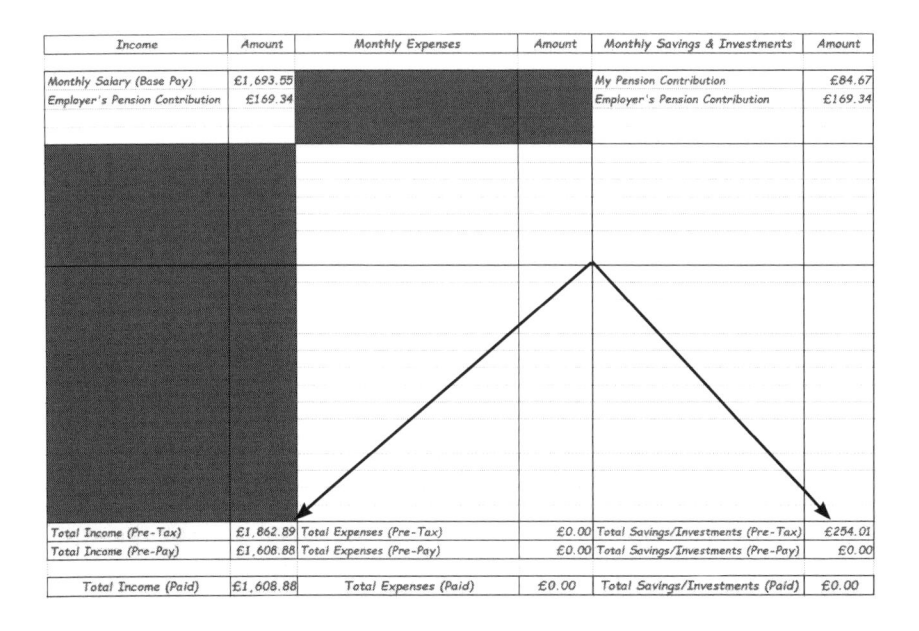

Income	Amount	Monthly Expenses	Amount	Monthly Savings & Investments	Amount
Monthly Salary (Base Pay)	£1,693.55			My Pension Contribution	£84.67
Employer's Pension Contribution	£169.34			Employer's Pension Contribution	£169.34
Total Income (Pre-Tax)	£1,862.89	Total Expenses (Pre-Tax)	£0.00	Total Savings/Investments (Pre-Tax)	£254.01
Total Income (Pre-Pay)	£1,608.88	Total Expenses (Pre-Pay)	£0.00	Total Savings/Investments (Pre-Pay)	£0.00
Total Income (Paid)	£1,608.88	Total Expenses (Paid)	£0.00	Total Savings/Investments (Paid)	£0.00

As you can see, technically Lloyd's monthly income or **Total Income (Pre-tax)** is **£1,862.89**, way more than we might have originally thought, as his employer pays an additional **10%** of his salary into his pension.

Whilst his **Monthly Savings & Investments** add up to **£254.01**.

However, if we can remember, there are still plenty of other deductions that happen before we get our precious money.

These deductions are your **pre-pay expenses**.

Any other deductions seen on your payslip should be inputted here, in the Orange Section, under the **Monthly Expenses Column**. (Tax, national insurance & student loan payments from the salary calculator if you had to use it)

Income	Amount	Monthly Expenses	Amount	Monthly Savings & Investments	Amount
Monthly Salary (Base Pay)	£1,693.55			My Pension Contribution	£84.67
Employer's Pension Contribution	£169.34			Employer's Pension Contribution	£169.34
		Tax	£112.28		
		National Insurance	£74.38		
		Worker's Union	£8.74		
Total Income (Pre-Tax)	£1,862.89	Total Expenses (Pre-Tax)	£0.00	Total Savings/Investments (Pre-Tax)	£254.01
Total Income (Pre-Pay)	£1,608.88	Total Expenses (Pre-Pay)	£195.40	Total Savings/Investments (Pre-Pay)	£0.00
Total Income (Paid)	£1,413.48	Total Expenses (Paid)	£0.00	Total Savings/Investments (Paid)	£0.00

As we learned earlier from studying his payslip, Lloyd is paying **£112.28** in tax, **£74.38** in national insurance contributions and **£8.74** for his workers' union fee. So, Lloyd has a total of **£195.40** in **pre-pay monthly expenses**.

Let's go back for a minute to get our head around this:

Initially, Lloyd had a total **pre-tax income** of **£1,862.89**- which includes his base pay and employer's pension contributions paid to him monthly.

When he subtracts out both his pension payments, he will arrive at his total **pre-pay income** of **£1,608.88**.

Income	Amount	Monthly Expenses	Amount	Monthly Savings & Investments	Amount
Monthly Salary (Base Pay)	£1,693.55			My Pension Contribution	£84.67
Employer's Pension Contribution	£169.34			Employer's Pension Contribution	£169.34
		Tax	£112.28		
		National Insurance	£74.38		
		Worker's Union	£8.74		
Total Income (Pre-Tax)	£1,862.89	Total Expenses (Pre-Tax)	£0.00	Total Savings/Investments (Pre-Tax)	£254.01
Total Income (Pre-Pay)	£1,608.88	Total Expenses (Pre-Pay)	£195.40	Total Savings/Investments (Pre-Pay)	£0.00
Total Income (Paid)	£1,413.48	Total Expenses (Paid)	£0.00	Total Savings/Investments (Paid)	£0.00

His **pre-pay income** can also be called his **gross pay** - or, as you know, **taxable income**.

So, Lloyd's tax (as well as his other **pre-pay** deductions) will be taken from this amount.

Hence, by subtracting all his deductions, Lloyd will arrive at the figure paid into his bank account: **£1,413.48**, which also happens to be... Yup, you guessed it. His **net pay**.

Income	Amount	Monthly Expenses	Amount	Monthly Savings & Investments	Amount
Monthly Salary (Base Pay)	£1,693.55			My Pension Contribution	£84.67
Employer's Pension Contribution	£169.34			Employer's Pension Contribution	£169.34
		Tax	£112.28		
		National Insurance	£74.38		
		Worker's Union	£8.74		
Total Income (Pre-Tax)	£1,862.89	Total Expenses (Pre-Tax)	£0.00	Total Savings/Investments (Pre-Tax)	£254.01
Total Income (Pre-Pay)	£1,608.88	Total Expenses (Pre-Pay)	£195.40	Total Savings/Investments (Pre-Pay)	£0.00
Total Income (Paid)	£1,413.48	Total Expenses (Paid)	£0.00	Total Savings/Investments (Paid)	£0.00

All this is great, but there is a chance you may be doing some additional saving and investing before you get paid but after you are taxed.

These tend to be in the form of schemes that encourage employees to save and invest their money, usually into the company that they work for.

If this is the case for you, and you are setting a bit aside before you're paid, you can input that into the **Orange Section** too, but this time under the **Monthly Savings & Investments Column**.

Income	Amount	Monthly Expenses	Amount	Monthly Savings & Investments	Amount
Monthly Salary (Base Pay)	£1,693.55			My Pension Contribution	£84.67
Employer's Pension Contribution	£169.34			Employer's Pension Contribution	£169.34
		Tax	£112.28		
		National Insurance	£74.38		
		Worker's Union	£8.74		
Total Income (Pre-Tax)	£1,862.89	Total Expenses (Pre-Tax)	£0.00	Total Savings/Investments (Pre-Tax)	£254.01
Total Income (Pre-Pay)	£1,608.88	Total Expenses (Pre-Pay)	£195.40	Total Savings/Investments (Pre-Pay)	£0.00
Total Income (Paid)	£1,413.48	Total Expenses (Paid)	£0.00	Total Savings/Investments (Paid)	£0.00

Now, I know that all this might seem overly complex, probably nobody has ever told you to record your finances in such a detailed way before.

However, wrapping your head around this and keeping a record of your whole financial position will help build the type of base that we are striving for.

There is so much going on with your money, before it even touches your account, that if you just recorded what happened after you're paid, you're only looking at half the picture.

Next, you will want to be logging what I call your **visible finances**.

These are any regular monthly expenses that you have.

Off the top of your head, you should know a couple of these already: your rent/mortgage payment, Netflix, car finance, and so on.

However, to be 100% certain that you have put down all your monthly expenses- without missing a word- you'll probably need a more systematic approach.

Go to your online banking app- or website- and look over the previous month's transactions.

There is no need to include the chocolate bar that you brought from the one-stop last week, only the regular payments.

Each month, these expenses are deducted from your account, whether automatically or voluntarily.

If you are unsure about capturing everything, look at the month prior to last. Then, compare the two, ensuring that you do not miss any payment.

When recording debt repayments, ensure you record the minimum monthly payment, rather than what you may be paying now.

Each one you find, log into **Red Section** of the **Monthly Expenses Column**.

Income	Amount	Monthly Expenses	Amount	Monthly Savings & Investments	Amount
Monthly Salary (Base Pay)	£1,693.55			My Pension Contribution	£84.67
Employer's Pension Contribution	£169.34			Employer's Pension Contribution	£169.34
		Tax	£112.28		
		National Insurance	£74.38		
		Worker's Union	£8.74		
Total Income (Pre-Tax)	£1,862.89	Total Expenses (Pre-Tax)	£0.00	Total Savings/Investments (Pre-Tax)	£254.01
Total Income (Pre-Pay)	£1,608.88	Total Expenses (Pre-Pay)	£195.40	Total Savings/Investments (Pre-Pay)	£0.00
Total Income (Paid)	£1,413.48	Total Expenses (Paid)	£0.00	Total Savings/Investments (Paid)	£0.00

Now, there is also section to record any regular **Monthly Savings & Investments** that you might be making after you've been paid, just here:

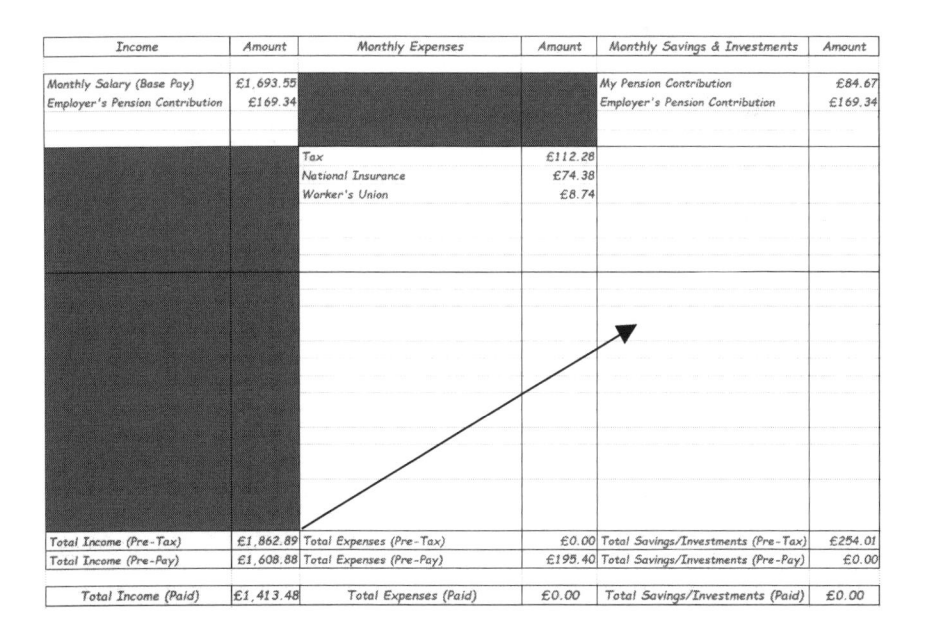

Income	Amount	Monthly Expenses	Amount	Monthly Savings & Investments	Amount
Monthly Salary (Base Pay)	£1,693.55			My Pension Contribution	£84.67
Employer's Pension Contribution	£169.34			Employer's Pension Contribution	£169.34
		Tax	£112.28		
		National Insurance	£74.38		
		Worker's Union	£8.74		
Total Income (Pre-Tax)	£1,862.89	Total Expenses (Pre-Tax)	£0.00	Total Savings/Investments (Pre-Tax)	£254.01
Total Income (Pre-Pay)	£1,608.88	Total Expenses (Pre-Pay)	£195.40	Total Savings/Investments (Pre-Pay)	£0.00
Total Income (Paid)	£1,413.48	Total Expenses (Paid)	£0.00	Total Savings/Investments (Paid)	£0.00

However, we don't want to do that just yet as what we're paying in here is likely to change later on in this book.

It might even be worth putting on hold any standing orders you have doing this automatically for the time being.

Let's catch back up with Lloyd and see what he's been up to!

Income	Amount	Monthly Expenses	Amount	Monthly Savings & Investments	Amount
Monthly Salary (Base Pay)	£1,693.55			My Pension Contribution	£84.67
Employer's Pension Contribution	£169.34			Employer's Pension Contribution	£169.34
		Tax	£112.28		
		National Insurance	£74.38		
		Worker's Union	£8.74		
		Rent Payment	£650.00		
		Council Tax	£120.59		
		Water	£38.52		
		Gas & Electric (Energy)	£85.10		
		Internet & TV	£45.16		
		Spotify	£9.99		
		Netflix	£8.99		
		Amazon Prime	£3.99		
		Mobile Phone Bill	£39.80		
		Playstation Plus	£6.99		
		Tinder Gold	£7.49		
		Car Finance	£75.00		
		Sainsbury's Credit Card (Min Payment)	£15.00		
		HSBC Credit Card (Min Payment)	£60.00		
Total Income (Pre-Tax)	£1,862.89	Total Expenses (Pre-Tax)	£0.00	Total Savings/Investments (Pre-Tax)	£254.01
Total Income (Pre-Pay)	£1,608.88	Total Expenses (Pre-Pay)	£195.40	Total Savings/Investments (Pre-Pay)	£0.00
Total Income (Paid)	£1,413.48	Total Expenses (Paid)	£1,166.62	Total Savings/Investments (Paid)	£0.00

Cor, go on, Lloyd. Your finances might not be the best, but you sure don't mess about.

Looking at this, though, we can see that Lloyd's got quite the number of monthly expenses on his plate.

But then, yours might be longer- and that's perfectly fine (for now...)

We can see a summary of his income through each stage of its journey.

After receiving a total income of **£1,862,89** Lloyd's left with just **£246.86** for the month, as shown to the right of your spreadsheet and in the table below:

Taxes	£186.66	10.02%
Expenses	£1,175.36	63.09%
Savings & Investments	£254.01	13.64%
Spending Money	£246.86	13.25%

Now this is better than nothing, but, when you factor in that his costs on commuting and groceries (which are also constant) are not included, neither are any daily lifestyle spending (i.e., that chocolate bar we mentioned earlier), things start to look a lot worse for Lloyd.

So, what can Lloyd do?

Frankly, Lloyd can improve his financial situation in two ways:

Either by spending less or making more.

The same applies to you.

For now though, I'm going to focus on helping you reduce your spending.

Why?

Because what's the point in making more if you don't curb how much money you spend?

It's no good earning a fortune if you spend a fortune.

How would you ever be able to retire?

Wealth is less about how much you earn and more about how much you keep.

Don't get me wrong- increasing your income is essential. In fact, it's so important that I plan on covering all that in the other books of this financial series.

But for the time being, here's where cutting down on your expenses and increasing your savings comes into the scene.

If you can muster enough discipline (which you must), you can eventually save enough to pay off any outstanding bad debt you may have, begin building wealth and free yourself from living from pay-check to pay-check.

Being in debt is becoming far too popular, and this might just be robbing you of your financial dream (whatever that might be).

As much as using your credit card gives you an edge in emergency situations, reckless use leads to more of a financial burden on you and your **cash flow**.

Cash flow describes the movement of money in and out of your account.

Being an all-encompassing term to describe the balance between what you receive and what you spend, your cash flow comprises two moving parts: cash received, and cash spent.

If you want to improve your cash flow- which your goal should be, you must lower the amount of money leaving your account.

Your monthly expenses can be classified into three major types:

Direct debits, standing orders and recurring payments- all of which can make you broke!

Direct Debits

Most people consider direct debits the simplest, safest, and most convenient way to make regular payments worldwide. Ranging from paying utility bills to council taxes, direct debits can be used to pay for nearly every single type of bill.

A direct debit authorises someone- usually an organisation- to collect payments of varying or fixed amounts from your account as and when they're due.

Standing Orders

A standing order is an instruction that you give your bank to send money to other people or organisations automatically.

A significant difference between these and direct debits is that you get to exercise more control over the amount taken.

Standing orders are pretty good for regular payments of fixed amounts such as paying rent.

So that you don't confuse standing orders for direct debits, here's the difference:

With direct debits, an organisation asks you- the payer- for permission to "draw" funds out of your account at recurring intervals.

However, standing orders are instructions issued from you to your bank to "push" funds to another person or organisation.

Recurring Payments

Recurring payments are most popular with subscription services such as Netflix and Spotify.

Your card is charged at the same time each month, usually on 30-day rolling contract, meaning most of the time, they can be cancelled at your leisure.

Cutting Your Bills

Depending on your position, it might be time to trim these down so that you only have essential monthly payments.

If you earn decent money and just want to be on top of your finances, then I'm not going to ask you to cancel a **£9.99** Netflix subscription.

However, those of you who are struggling with bad debt, these might be the sort of sacrifices that you need to make.

So why shouldn't you enjoy decent entertainment?

If you owe someone else money, then anything you spend outside of basic necessities is money that could be paying that off, in turn leading you to be able to watch that new show, stress-free.

Unfortunately, ole Lloyd here falls into this category.

Now, scan through your spreadsheet and separate the wheat from the chaff.

Here, you must engage in the emotion-less editing of your monthly expenses.

What are your needs? What are your wants?

Do you think you can survive without some of those expenses- for instance, do you really need tinder gold?

Assess your financial position honestly and decide what you feel can and can't stay.

While some of your expenses can be removed, there are some expenses that you shouldn't really lay your hands on, i.e., necessary expenses.

Necessary expenses include things such as your rent, water and council taxes. Since we are in a modern society, things like energy and internet bills are also essential.

Once you've sorted out the essentials, mark out the things that can be removed.

Before going ahead and actually cancelling them, ensure you are out of contract, otherwise you may get in trouble and have to pay a fine.

Believe me, I know just how tough doing this can be.

You're thinking, I love music; how will I ever cope without Spotify?

The truth is, it's not about the **£9.99** you're saving; it's about what that **£9.99** means.

It's a promise you make to yourself, a promise that is with you every day.

The promise that you're doing this for a reason, you're doing this to get to where you want to be.

And so, after some pretty tough decisions, Lloyd has chosen that the following payments are non-essential: Netflix, Spotify, Amazon Prime, PlayStation Plus and Tinder Gold.

Again, this is because Lloyd's in a pretty unfortunate position of not earning a lot, and having some bad debt.

If Lloyd can cope without these, then you probably can do too.

Difficult? Yes.

Impossible? No.

In the financial world, there is a term known as **delayed gratification**. It is the act of postponing or denying oneself of momentary pleasure/gain in view of a greater reward later on.

If your goal is to clear your debt - then you must be willing to make the necessary sacrifices.

Remember the dream you thought of earlier? Well, this is one of those times where you're going to have to make a tough call and might feel like giving up.

Let's hope you make the decision that'll give you that greater reward in the long run.

So, cancel all the pointless sh*t, get all that junk off your spreadsheet, and see how much money you've saved!

Let's take a look and see how Lloyd's spreadsheet now looks:

Income	Amount	Monthly Expenses	Amount	Monthly Savings & Investments	Amount
Monthly Salary (Base Pay)	£1,693.55			My Pension Contribution	£84.67
Employer's Pension Contribution	£169.34			Employer's Pension Contribution	£169.34
		Tax	£112.28		
		National Insurance	£74.38		
		Worker's Union	£8.74		
		Rent Payment	£650.00		
		Council Tax	£120.59		
		Water	£38.52		
		Gas & Electric (Energy)	£85.10		
		Internet & TV	£45.16		
		Mobile Phone Bill	£39.80		
		Car Finance	£75.00		
		Sainsbury's Credit Card (Min Payment)	£15.00		
		HSBC Credit Card (Min Payment)	£60.00		
Total Income (Pre-Tax)	£1,862.89	Total Expenses (Pre-Tax)	£0.00	Total Savings/Investments (Pre-Tax)	£254.01
Total Income (Pre-Pay)	£1,608.88	Total Expenses (Pre-Pay)	£195.40	Total Savings/Investments (Pre-Pay)	£0.00
Total Income (Paid)	£1,413.48	Total Expenses (Paid)	£1,129.17	Total Savings/Investments (Paid)	£0.00

That certainly, looks a lot better visually, however, he's only been able to save **£37.45**.

This isn't hundreds, but then, this is a great start!

Minor changes create ripple effects.

Take an Amazon Prime subscription for instance.

Granted, by cancelling this subscription, we save **£3.99** a month.

However, by not having access to next day delivery, perhaps we might think twice before buying yet another pack lunch box.

The same applies for Tinder Gold. It means fewer fancy restaurants and buying clothes we can't afford to impress people we don't like.

So, you see- the list is endless. In personal finance, small changes bring about a big impact.

Look, I know that Lloyd might not have all the same expenses as you, but you can use the same principles that he's applied to sort out what's unnecessary from what's important.

Saving isn't a one-time activity- it is a culture, a habit that you nurture. So, it's okay to begin small- in tens.

If you don't learn the culture of savings now, when do you want to do so?

Your Maze Checklist:

By now, you should know that simply finishing reading a chapter isn't enough. Sorry!

1. Record your **Total Earnings & Deductions** in your spreadsheet's relevant rows and columns.

If you are stuck anywhere, refer back to the previous pages of this chapter or get in touch with me. (will@the-money-maze.co.uk)

2. Analyse your transactions and record your visible finances (your regular automatic payments).

3. Go through your bills and pick which ones can go.

4. Cancel them and then see how much you've saved!

CHAPTER FIVE

What About The Things I Just have To Pay?
Saving On The Unavoidable Stuff

Now I'm hoping that you've cut out all the stuff you can't afford. If you haven't done so, you should definitely go back and get this sorted before reading on.

Done? Great.

Now that's been dealt with, you will probably notice that you are still forking out a huge chunk of your monthly income on your regular expenses.

You've still got quite a bit of work to do in order to increase your savings potential. So, what should you do now?

Well, your answer is in this chapter. Lucky you.

To reduce your expenses further to increase how much you save, you can do so by attempting to get the best-deals-possible on the remaining "extremely necessary" stuff.

Saving on your rent and mortgage payments- is that possible?

Yes.

Since your rent or mortgage payment is most likely your largest expense, saving in this area can have a significant effect on your personal finances.

With this in mind, how can this be done?

The best and not always the most popular or feasible answer is to consider getting a roommate.

This is probably the quickest and most effective method for saving on your accommodation cost.

Luckily, doing so won't just cut down your housing bill- the effect can be widespread.

Ranging from your energy to internet costs, you could save a ridiculous amount of your monthly income if these were shared.

Whether you are able to do this or not, you should still spend some time researching the average rent in your area- just to have a background check on if you are being overcharged.

If you find this to be true, approach your landlord- not in an angry manner- but with a rather friendly approach and start a conversation about what you are paying.

After all, a reliable and good tenant is a perfect example of one of those non-tangible assets we spoke about earlier.

In addition, it is crucial that you understand your rights and responsibilities as a tenant, so you do not open up your wallet to costs that you shouldn't be paying. For instance, your landlord is always responsible for:

- Heating repairs
- Electrical wiring

- The property's structure and exterior.

- Sinks, basins, and other sanitary fittings such as the pipes.

- Any damage caused when attempting repairs.

However, some repairs are entirely your responsibility. For instance, if you mistakenly damage your flat, you've got to fix that. Sorry.

Damages caused by family and friends are also your cross to carry.

As for mortgages, well, here's where it gets a little bit technical.

Getting a mortgage might be one of your greatest financial commitments, so it is essential that you get this right.

Your decision here will go on to affect your income for decades to come. So, while you may have a rush of excitement about getting your own home, you must understand how the market works- including the different types of mortgages and which is best for you.

The best way to save on your mortgage is through the use of an independent mortgage broker.

The market is simply too complicated, and you can make mistakes without professional eyes overseeing your decisions.

Having an expert scour the market for you could save you hundreds of pounds every month, increasing your ability to save and start amassing some real wealth.

When you want to buy a property, your estate agent will most likely push that you use their own in-house mortgage broker. As a piece of advice, don't.

Hiring an independent mortgage broker is far better than going with an affiliated one. To get a reliable mortgage broker, the best answer I can give you is to reach out to your family and friends for a recommendation.

When you finally get a certified mortgage broker, they'll discuss the different types of mortgages with you and see which one is best suited to your income and lifestyle.

In brief, there are two primary ways through which you can repay what you owe: a capital repayment mortgage or an interest-only mortgage.

Capital Repayment Mortgages

In this kind of mortgage, your monthly repayment is calculated so that the interest on the mortgage (for that moment) and some part of the actual debt is paid off monthly- so that after the mortgage term, you will have repaid it all.

When you begin making monthly payments at first, you will notice that most of your money is swallowed by the interests on the actual debt.

However, as you pay off the debt little by little, the principal amount will decrease- and so will the interest.

While in your early years, the monthly payments might go towards paying off the interest, in the later years, most of your repayment will go towards paying off the initial sum borrowed.

Interest-Only Mortgages

The major difference between an interest-only mortgage and a capital repayment mortgage is that the amount you'll pay only covers the interest.

So, you will still owe the amount you initially borrowed at the end of the mortgage term (e.g., 25 years), and have to still pay this as a lump sum when the term is over.

People who go for this kind of mortgage usually have a separate plan to pay off the debt by the end of the term.

In fact, before you can receive this type of mortgage, you must prove to the lender that you've set up a system that will enable you to pay off the actual cost of the property when the term is over.

Whether in a repayment mortgage or interest-only mortgage, the amount of interest you pay could be fixed or variable.

Mortgages with a fixed interest rate are known as **fixed-rate mortgages**, while mortgages with variable interest rates are called **variable-rate mortgages**. Shock.

With a **fixed-rate mortgage**, the lender usually offers an incentive in the form of a special interest rate, which lasts for just a short term.

This interest rate remains the same over the period known as the **incentive period**.

Each fixed-rate mortgage has its own incentive period- ranging from two to fifteen years.

When this period ends, you will be transferred to the **standard variable rate (SVR)**, which – in most cases- will be higher than the fixed interest rate. (I'll talk more about this subsequently).

A significant advantage of this kind of mortgage is having a consistent mortgage budget due to the absence of interest fluctuations.

On the hand, a disadvantage is that if the general market interest rates fall, the amount of interest that you're paying pay won't move an inch.

As the name suggests, the rates aren't always the same for **variable-rate mortgages** and could change anytime.

In fact, it is advisable that you have savings set aside to address any sudden changes in the interest rate when going for this kind of mortgage.

Although not the sole factor, the U.K. economy plays a massive role in defining the rates.

Variable-rate mortgages come in three types: tracker mortgages, standard variable mortgages and discount rate mortgages.

Tracker Mortgages

Have you ever seen a remora fish move with a shark?

If you haven't, quickly search a picture on Google; it will help you understand this concept.

Done?

Okay.

In the U.K., whenever the Bank of England lends to other banks, it does so using the interest rate known as the **base rate**.

Take this to be the Shark. The banks then lend to you with an interest rate, known as your mortgage rate.

Take this be the remora fish.

You will notice that the remora fish clings to the shark as it moves.

Likewise, your interest (or mortgage) rate clings to the base rate in tracker mortgages, plus a few percent.

If the bank rate increases by **0.4%**, so will your interest rate.

This kind of mortgage brings some level of transparency and certainty- your interest rate won't be affected by the lender's considerations but, instead, just by economic factors.

Standard Variable Mortgages

I've already mentioned this mortgage type when discussing fixed-rate ones earlier. But now is time for some more detail...

After the incentive period- if you go for a fixed-rate mortgage- you will automatically be moved to the rate of the lender, known as the **standard variable rate** (SVR).

So, here's how it goes: each lender has an SVR which they can move whenever they like.

Although they might claim to follow the Bank of England's base rate, this is done roughly- meaning, SVR's could range from about **2-5%** above the base rate.

Indeed, this kind of mortgage can be seen as slightly risker, as your lender can up your payments based on commercial reasons.

Here, the interest you pay can go up or down at any time, leaving you vulnerable.

Although, there is in fact no early repayment charges, which is great if you are planning on overpaying or paying off your remaining balance at any time; say you come into a large sum of inheritance.

Discount-Rate Mortgages

This kind of mortgage involves a discount off the lender's standard variable rate. This discount usually lasts for a short period of time (compared to the mortgage term), typically 2-3 years.

Here, it is advisable to look around before settling for a discount rate- sometimes, lower discount rates are better than higher discount rates.

For instance, if BANK C offers a **2%** discount off an SVR of **6%**, you will pay an interest rate of **4%**.

On the other hand, if another bank, BANK D, offers a discount of **1.5%** off an SVR of **5%**, you will pay an interest rate of **3.5%**.

Hence, even though BANK C offers a higher discount, in reality, BANK D is the better option.

Similar to fixed-rate mortgages, after the discount period ends, you'll get transferred to the lender's standard variable rate.

At this point, most people consider it a better option to **re-mortgage** when the discount period (for discount-rate mortgages) or incentive period (for fixed-rate mortgages) runs out, than continue on the SVR.

Re-mortgaging simply means using a new mortgage to pay off an existing mortgage.

Don't confuse this with a **second charge mortgage** which refers to taking out another mortgage that co-exists with your current mortgage deal.

Usually, when you want to re-mortgage, you'll need to approach a new lender who has a better deal compared to your existing one.

Among its several other benefits, re-mortgaging allows you to access better interest rates and perhaps, provides you with more flexibility.

The subject of re-mortgaging is complex; the mechanics involved can be very confusing, hence, the use of a mortgage broker again is a good idea.

This is why you should; if you are in the market to buy a home, speak with our very own in-house mortgage broker here at The Money Maze!

Haha, almost got you.

Getting a mortgage is a huge step- and it's crucial that you make the right choice. In doing so, you will pay less every month and own a house at the end of the mortgage term.

Council Tax

Let's talk about council taxes. Yes, I know, another form of bloody tax. However, these ones are paid to your local council for the services provided, such as libraries and rubbish collection.

Usually, your council tax is paid in 10 monthly instalments, followed by 2 months of not making any payment (February and March).

However, some councils will allow you to spread this tax over 12 months rather than 10.

If you're 18 and over, and either own or rent a property, you will have to pay council tax.

But how's your council tax even calculated?

Simple- by using these three factors:

- The valuation band for your home (which varies in Scotland).
- The amount your local council charges for that particular valuation band (this varies across different local councils).
- Whether you are eligible for a discount or a total exemption.

There are several circumstances where you'll be able to pay less on your council tax bill. This is because the standard bill is calculated off 2 adults living under the same roof.

You can actually get 25% off your bill if you live alone.

You don't have to pay any council tax if everyone in your household, including you, is a full-time student.

Hurray!

However, it'll involve some work on your front I'm afraid, and so to apply for your discounts it is best to visit:

https://www.gov.uk/apply-for-council-tax-discount

You can also check and see if you have been put on the correct council tax band here too. If you think you are overpaying, you'll need a review. And, if this comes out positive, you may be entitled to thousands of pounds. (P.S.: You could also be moved to a higher band.)

You win some, you lose some.

Water

Would you believe me if I told you that you might be spending too much on water?

Or are you one of those people who consider trying to cut their water bills an impossible task?

If you are, I'm here to challenge you (not to a boxing match).

The truth is that although many consider trying to cut their water bill a dead end, it is possible to save up to hundreds of pounds on it.

The first problem you might have realised is that you can't switch between water providers. This leads many to believe that if they can't switch providers- like you can do in the case of gas and electricity- they can't save on water.

If you can address how you are billed however, you might be able to reduce this cost.

Generally, you can be billed in two ways- by either paying a fixed amount (depending on the size of your home) or by paying for only what you use through the use a water metre.

So, should you swap to a water metre?

Here's a general rule of thumb: If there are fewer people in your house than bedrooms- or the same number- consider getting a water metre.

Whether a water metre will help you or not is dependent on your water usage. To check if you are a good fit, try out this calculator:

https://www.ccwater.org.uk/watermetercalculator/

You'll be able to get an estimate what your water bill could be if you chose to be charged based on your usage.

Then, if the difference between your current billing and the estimated bill is financially worthwhile, go for it!

To get one, check your provider's website. There's usually an application form there- worst-case scenario, give them a call.

A water metre is typically free to install in England and Wales, and most places already have one.

However, it is not free in Scotland (actually, it could be a little expensive) - so it might be better to stick to the estimated payments that you're already paying.

If you live in Northern Ireland, the good news is then you don't need a metre- domestic water use is free of charge!

If you decide to switch over to a metre, or are already on one, here are some tips to keep your bill low:

- Did you know that a running tap could consume up to nine litres of water every minute? Now you do. When brushing your teeth, turn off the tap.

- Minimise how long you stay in the bathroom. It is estimated that a 5-minute shower uses half the volume than of a standard bath.

- If you have a garden, use a watering can rather than sprinklers or hosepipes. You could save as much as 500-1000 litres of water per hour.

- Could there be a leak in your internal plumbing? Inspect your property regularly.

- Have you ever considered saving rainwater for watering your gardens? Get a water butt to collect rainwater off your roof.

- Rather than using a running tap to wash fruits and vegetables, get a bowl. Use the wastewater to then water your plants.

- Before using your dishwasher or washing machine, ensure you've got a full load.

- When installed in your toilet cistern, water-saving devices could potentially help you save between one to three litres of water each time you flush.

- Fill a jug of water and put it in the fridge whenever you feel like having a cool drink.

Gas and Electricity

It's practically impossible to live in our world today without access to gas and electricity. From helping us eat to giving us access to social media, it cuts across all areas of our lives.

Unlike the water sector, you're to shop around for different suppliers- who initially buy energy from the wholesale market and supply it directly to you- the consumer.

Briefly, let me give you an overview of how the energy sector in the U.K. works.

So, you've got three significant stops: Energy generation, energy transportation and energy sale.

Energy can be generated via the use of non-renewable and renewable sources. Non-renewable sources include coal and gas, while renewable sources include wind and solar power.

Once generated, the energy is transported via the national grid, which is composed of two channels: transmission and distribution.

While transmission refers to energy transport via long distances, distribution refers to more local and short distances.

Then lastly, energy sale involves selling energy from suppliers (who buy the generated energy from the wholesale market) and selling it to everyday consumers like yourself.

In the U.K., there are up to sixty of such suppliers in the market.

However, the energy market is dominated by the "big six":

- Centrica
- EDF Energy
- OVO
- Scottish Power
- E.ON
- nPower

So, what determines the price you pay for the energy you consume?

The tariff you pay. There are two types of tariffs- a variable rate tariff or a fixed rate tariff.

With a **variable rate tariff**, the price you pay per unit of energy isn't constant, while in a **fixed rate tariff**, the price you pay is set for an agreed period.

Variable-rate tariffs tend to be the default tariffs.

So, if you've never switched suppliers, you are most likely on this. However, the thing is: fixed-rate tariffs tend to be cheaper than their counterparts.

As for paying your bills, there are four ways this can be done: monthly direct debits, quarterly direct debit, payment on receipt of the bill, and the through the use of a prepayment meter.

Monthly Direct Debits

Remember that we talked about direct debits earlier, right? Here, on the same date – or around the same date- every month, an amount comes out of your account.

Hence, you need to ensure that you have enough in your account to cover the cost.

An advantage or disadvantage (depending on how you view this) of using this method means that your monthly payment might not precisely be enough to cover your energy bill- you'll either overpay or underpay.

This is because seasons change- and with that comes a fluctuating energy bill, and also sometimes you forget to turn the heating off, only to come home after work to start sweating profusely.

Your energy supplier will need to ramp up your monthly direct debit to keep you out of the reds if you regularly underpay. Your supplier is also entitled to prevent you from switching until your bill with them is settled.

However, on the bright side, if you regularly overpay, you can build up credit on your account.

You can then choose either of these paths when you've got credit: you could either allow your monthly payment to go down or leave your monthly payment unchanged while using the credit to supplement in months when your energy usage goes up.

If you want to switch suppliers and have credit, make sure you get this back before leaving.

Quarterly Direct Debit

Similar to paying monthly direct debits, except this time, you pay for three months' worth of energy use at once.

This can be risky as you may not make adequate preparations for the payment if you forget it is coming. Hence, many people instead go for the monthly plan.

Payment on Receipt of Bill

If direct debits are just not your thing and you prefer to make payments online, by phone, by cash, or via a cheque at your bank, then this might be for you.

Every quarter, an energy bill - which gives an accurate reflection of your energy usage for the past three months- arrives at your doorstep. And then, well you pay it.

Prepayment Meter

To begin with, this is the most expensive way you could possibly settle your gas and electricity bill.

But just for knowledge's sake, let's talk about it.

This is a "pay-as-you-go" kind of technique. Here, you pay for your energy usage upfront by using a token or a top-up key.

Some landlords tend to go for this because they don't want their tenants accumulating large energy debts.

Hence, it makes sense for tenants to pay upfront. If, as a tenant, you don't like this and you'd like to switch from prepaid to the direct debit method, speak to your landlord.

Switching suppliers still remains one of the best ways to save on gas and electricity.

Why?

Well, usually, suppliers offer considerable discounts to new customers. So, you could save as much as hundreds of pounds a year for the simple task of changing suppliers.

Despite this, nearly 11 million people have never done this.

If you are one of these people, listen- or rather, read- closely because this is a gold mine.

So, here's how it works: When you initially sign up with an energy supplier, you'll will be tied up with a contract ranging from 12 months to 24 months if you opt for a fixed-rate tariff.

Within this period, you will pay a fixed amount per unit of energy you consume.

Regardless of fluctuations in energy prices, your energy billing will remain constant. However, switching to another supplier attracts a penalty fee.

When this contract period ends, you are automatically moved to the standard variable tariff.

Once this happens, you have two options: you could either strike a new deal with your current supplier so you can be moved back to a fixed-term tariff (which is usually lower than a standard variable tariff), or you could grab a new deal with a new supplier without paying a penalty fee.

This would be the best time to switch!

Before switching providers, however, ensure that you look around for the best deal. There's really no point in changing if your new contract is the same as the current price that you are paying.

Internet & T.V.

If you've been using the same broadband service for over a year or two, I can also help you save on your internet and T.V. spending.

Okay, so here's the thing: It is very common to see broadband services offer attractive deals to new customers- so that they can have a bite.

This comes in the form of a contract- which, in most cases, lasts for about 18 to 24 months. So, your bills will be really cheap (well, comparably cheap) within this period, but you can't dump the service midway through, unless you want to pay a hefty exit fee.

When your contract eventually ends, your monthly payment usually ramps up (rather heavily). So, it's always advisable to switch service providers once your term is up.

If you want to save money on your internet and T.V. usage by switching though, you must compare home broadband deals.

If you are still tied to a contract presently and want to move on to greener pastures in months to come, begin looking for a better deal now.

When switching, the general rule of thumb is that it takes about two weeks to connect a new service.

However, I don't imply that you'd stay offline for two weeks- if you were, how would you be able to keep up with the Kardashians?

You should expect to spend between 30 minutes- 1 hour offline while the change takes place. Of course, if your switch requires an engineer visit, this time limit might be extended.

To save you some sweat, let me run you through the steps to make a switch:

- Begin by checking for available broadband packages within your postcode. A key thing to look out for is internet speed. The faster, the better.

- Compare the broadband packages you come across. Do this by using the same factors across the board- what's the budget on the table? What are your usage habits? If you have a couple of people living with you in your household- do you need an ultrafast broadband speed? If you live alone- what speed would be okay for just you?

Once you get your priorities right, it's easier to handpick the packages in line with what you want.

Once you are sure about the provider you want to switch to, notify that provider. From this point onwards, your new provider will handle the entire process, including the cancellation of your old contract.

As a piece of advice, you should keep the subscription details you receive from your new provider- which typically includes your prices and contract end date; it will definitely prove helpful in the future.

Lastly, some providers charge a connection fee. So, when signing up, don't skip the terms and conditions section- even though you usually would under normal circumstances.

Mobile Phones

It goes without saying – a mobile phone is a must.

So, here's how the mobile phone industry operates: you can easily bag a new phone on the market with two payment methods- you could either pay a contract or get a sim-only deal.

A **mobile phone contract** simply refers to an agreement where you pay a single monthly fee for a fixed period – usually ranging between 12 and 24 months.

A percentage of this monthly fee covers part-payment of the handset, while the remainder gives you an allowance for calls, data, and texts.

On the other hand, when you opt for a **sim-only deal**, although you'll still be placed on the monthly payment regimen, the payments you make only cover calls, data, and text costs.

Meaning you'll need to buy the phone outright.

In the long run, monthly contracts cost more. So, it's usually wiser to save up to buy a new phone outright- and then opt for a sim-only deal- than to enter a mobile phone contract.

Here are three other rules you shouldn't forget when it comes to saving on your phone bill:

- Hold your old phone for a bit longer than normal. The average person may get a new mobile phone every two years. Instead, hold on to your phone for about three to four years. This could potentially save you hundreds of pounds.

- Always opt to buy a phone that will hold its value. This is where iPhones have the upper hand.

- When you get a new phone, keep the phone in good condition. Again, a no-brainer but an important rule as it will result in a higher re-sale value.

Car Insurance

Lloyd paid his car insurance upfront last year.

However, that's not always the case.

Your car insurance could be eating deep into your monthly finances.

To begin with, you should put in mind that car insurances are cheaper when you pay annually compared to paying monthly.

As monthly payments usually incur interest- which results in you paying way more overall.

So, begin saving for your car insurance months ahead so that you can go for the annual option.

Research has shown that securing a new deal 20-26 days before your renewal date can get you the best possible price.

Lastly, you should read all the terms and conditions of the insurance to know exactly what's covered in the insurance policy.

Asides from this preventing you from spending your personal cash on something that's covered, it also protects you from any "nasty" surprises.

Boring, I know! But essential, yes. Saving on the stuff you have to pay regardless is a great way to reduce your monthly spending significantly.

Just look at Lloyd:

Taxes	£186.66	10.02%
Expenses	£1,021.85	54.85%
Savings & Investments	£254.01	13.64%
Spending Money	£400.37	21.49%

You'll see he has moved from having **£284.31** leftover after his monthly bills to having **£400.37** - not bad right?

Income	Amount	Monthly Expenses	Amount	Monthly Savings & Investments	Amount
Monthly Salary (Base Pay)	£1,693.55			My Pension Contribution	£84.67
Employer's Pension Contribution	£169.34			Employer's Pension Contribution	£169.34
		Tax	£112.28		
		National Insurance	£74.38		
		Worker's Union	£8.74		
		Rent Payment	£650.00		
		Council Tax	£80.99		
		Water	£22.21		
		Gas & Electric (Energy)	£72.92		
		Internet & TV	£26.99		
		Mobile Phone Bill	£10.00		
		Car Finance	£75.00		
		Sainsbury's Credit Card	£15.00		
		HSBC Credit Card	£60.00		
Total Income (Pre-Tax)	£1,862.89	Total Expenses (Pre-Tax)	£0.00	Total Savings/Investments (Pre-Tax)	£254.01
Total Income (Pre-Pay)	£1,608.88	Total Expenses (Pre-Pay)	£195.40	Total Savings/Investments (Pre-Pay)	£0.00
Total Income (Paid)	£1,413.48	Total Expenses (Paid)	£1,013.11	Total Savings/Investments (Paid)	£0.00

To do this, first he extended his council tax payments over 12 months- rather than the traditional 10 and then redeemed his **25%** discount for living alone.

This reduced his bill down from **£121.59** to **£80.99**.

He then arranged for his water usage to be billed using a water metre and applied all the water conservation tips that I mentioned earlier.

This cut his water bill from **£38.52** to **£22.21**.

Lloyd also discovered that his phone contract had expired. So, rather than opting for a new phone, he got a cheap sim-only deal at **£10.00** a month.

While at work, Lloyd's friend told him about a broadband provider that had a banging deal going on for new customer's and another that could save him some cash on his energy bill.

So, he decided to take the switch and boom! He saved **£30.35** in the process.

So, that's Lloyd's report. What's yours?

Your Maze Checklist:

First all, well done for getting here, this chapter was a bit dull I know.

Good news is things should get a little more fun and interactive as we move forward, but now it's time for your list of things to do.

Don't you dare move to the next chapter without doing these (just kidding, but really, your understanding of this chapter is crucial for the next):

> **1**. Go through your expenses and apply newfound knowledge.
>
> This might involve a lot of phone calls and hold times, but don't worry this book will still be waiting for you after it's all sorted.
>
> **2**. Update your spreadsheet to reflect all your changes and look how much you now have left!
>
> Bonus points if you can beat Lloyd's savings of **£116.06** in total across both chapters!

CHAPTER SIX

What To Do With What's Left?
A Bit On Budgeting

We've come a long way so far and made some serious savings.

However, although it's great to do this, we're only halfway there, as we need to also understand how to spend what's left.

If you want to go far financially, you need to close these additional leaks which might be affecting your pocket even more.

Funnily enough, this just so happens to be what this chapter is about- closing those leaks and understanding how to keep some of what you've managed to hold of, post expenses.

First, I want you to understand the difference between two extremely important terms: Needs and wants.

Needs Vs. Wants: The age-long battle for your finances.

Your **financial needs** are essential for your survival. This includes things like food for your tummy and transport to work.

On the other hand, your **financial wants** are cravings within your soul that help you have fun and enjoy life.

Talk about your desire to spend the weekend in the Bahamas, or better still, take your fiancé to the most exquisite restaurant in town.

And- as though in a tug of war match- your needs and wants are battling it out for your attention.

When we are logical, we let our needs have the upper hand.

But, when we get into our feelings (especially after seeing those cute Instagram pictures with striking captions), our wants win.

While it is incredibly natural to want both, you must understand how to divide your hard-earned cash amongst these age-long rivals.

The most common method to do so is through **budgeting**.

No doubt, this term isn't new to you. You've probably heard many gurus talk about it- but I have always found budgeting extremely tedious.

So, I came up with a onetime way to settle the battle between my needs and my wants- a **semi-budget**.

Semi-budgets: would they work for me?

The principle is simple: Rather than budgeting for each and every category of expenditure, i.e., eating out, nights on the town, gifts, shopping and so on.

Instead, you give yourself an all-encompassing budget, to which you can spend however you like, derived from separating your spending into four main categories:

Needs, **necessities**, **wants** and the '**oh f*ck why did I do that category**' (**OFWDIDT** for short).

Necessities refer to anything that isn't essential to living your life but are important when functioning in society, i.e., getting your haircut.

OFWDIDT is pretty self-explanatory (anything you wasted your money on).

Let's explain this a little better:

The idea is if you want to spend lavishly on a new designer pair of shoes, fine, go-ahead mate.

But you may start to feel the pain somewhere else, like maybe having to spend the night drinking water and wishing the shoes were actually food (no hard feelings...)

So, rather than creating smaller budgets (that would be hard to remember), a singular all-in-one "spending" budget, which is in a separate account is a much easier and less time-consuming way of managing your money.

How's that sound? Pretty banging if you'd ask me.

How to create your semi-budget

To create one, you'll need to look at the last three months of your transactions- excluding your regular monthly expenses.

Go to your online banking app and expand the transaction history section to provide a 90-day view.

This way you can work out the average you are spending.

If you just looked at last month and you had a particular high cost, i.e., buying a festival ticket, you might think you spend loads, when in actual fact, you're not quite as trigger happy with the buy button as you may have otherwise thought.

All this is great Will, but what am I actually supposed to be looking for?

Another top question, well all we need to know for now is how much you spent and what it was on?

Was it on a **need**, a **necessity**, a **want**, or you guessed it, **oh f*ck why did I do that?**

You may have also noticed if you're as observant as Sherlock Holmes that I haven't asked you to record the date. Reason being, what would be the point?

I've seen some people even log the time of the transaction; God only knows why. In fact, ... If you know why, I'd love to hear from you.

First person to give me a valid answer gets a free copy of my next book.

Anyway, moving back to topic, you'll want to log each transaction down on the **Monthly Expenditure Tab** of your Money Maze Spreadsheet, like so:

Amount	Purpose
£9.99	Want

TOTAL	£9.99	AVERAGE	£3.33
Need	£0.00	Per Month	£0.00
Necessary	£0.00	Per Month	£0.00
Want	£9.99	Per Month	£3.33
OFWDIDT	£0.00	Per Month	£0.00

MY TOTAL SPENDING BUDGET

My Debt Line	£400.37

Needs	
Necessary	
Wants	
Oh Dear	

TOTAL	£0.00
LEFT OVER	£400.37

At ten past twelve on the 1st of August 2021, Lloyd was craving some snacks. So, he took his coat, hopped down the street to a Tortilla restaurant, and grabbed some food and drink.

All you can see however, is that he spent **£9.99** on a **want**. And really, that's all that matters.

Recording a time and place can add too much emotion to each transaction, and therefore might make it harder to justify limiting spending in certain areas.

These are problems that we don't want. We want to be able to look at our finances in black and white and make tough decisions where necessary.

Lloyd then continued inputting the rest of his transactions.

By the end, Lloyd was very bored but also delighted that he didn't have to do any maths again because his spreadsheet automatically told him how much he had spent on average across this period, as seen in the table to the upper right.

Amount	Purpose
£9.99	Want
£15.14	Want
£14.35	Need
£29.54	Need
£31.74	Want
£5.99	Necessary
£1.20	Want
£60.00	OFWDIDT
£2.00	Need
£78.00	Want
£4.20	Need
£1.30	Need
£7.64	Want
£8.85	OFWDIDT
£10.99	Want
£26.30	Want
£13.74	Want
£1.00	Necessary

TOTAL	£1,821.93	AVERAGE	£607.31
Need	£694.47	Per Month	£231.49
Necessary	£155.79	Per Month	£51.93
Want	£712.14	Per Month	£237.38
OFWDIDT	£259.53	Per Month	£86.51

MY TOTAL SPENDING BUDGET

My Debt Line	£400.37
Needs	
Necessary	
Wants	
Oh Dear	
TOTAL	£0.00
LEFT OVER	£400.37

Looking at Lloyd here as an example, he has spent **£1,821.93** for the entire 90-day period, which works out at **£607.31** per month.

The goal of this exercise is to check that this is in fact lower than what he had remaining after his bills.

Which, unfortunately, means that Lloyd has failed with flying colours.

As he only had **£400.37** remaining, as shown in the table

labelled **Debt Line**, and that's even after culling his monthly expenses!

Your debt line is the absolute minimum you can spend in a month without the need for overtime, bonuses and/or debt.

So, Lloyd, and possibly you too, need to find a way to bring your average spending lower than whatever you have left, post bills (your debt-line).

For those that are under this already, then you're in a great place.

It's now time to keep going, even if you thought you've won at this book and were thinking about now heading down to the pub.

I mean, if getting out of debt is your only goal, then who am I to argue with that, but for those who want to begin to amess wealth, you're still going to want to address your spending habits.

If we go back to Lloyd, we can see that he is currently overspending by **£206.94** every month.

£400.37 – £607.31 = -£206.94

So, how can Lloyd (and you) reduce this?

An easy place to start, is by looking at his needs:

Needs

As long as what you spend on your needs is below your debt line, you're going to be just fine!

However, if what you spend on your needs alone is above this, we get into the tough territory.

Not impossible, though; at this point, it might be worth considering your options and possibly looking to secure a secondary job.

I can't begin to imagine the circumstances that have led to this, nor will I pretend that they don't matter.

All I know is that this sort of thing won't be forever, and the sooner you start, the sooner it'll be over.

Don't feel afraid to reach out to me should you want to get in touch about your personal situation.

TOTAL	£1,821.93	AVERAGE	£607.31
Need	£694.47	Per Month	£231.49
Necessary	£155.79	Per Month	£51.93
Want	£712.14	Per Month	£237.38
OFWDIDT	£259.53	Per Month	£86.51

On a lighter touch, on average Lloyd is currently dishing out **£231.49** for his needs each month, as shown on this table, to the right of your spreadsheet.

And this is great because it is far below his debt line.

Even though that's good, it won't be harmful to look deeper into these needs and still try to eliminate some extra stuff, right?

Needs may differ from person to person, but I think we can all agree that groceries and transport tend to be the main culprits.

You may be able to reduce spending in these areas by:

- Focus on buying ingredients, spending time cooking- rather than eating ready-made meals or frozen foods.

- You could also try shopping at alternate supermarkets such as Lidl or Aldi, as a shopping basket could be up to 20% cheaper than if you shopped at Tesco or Sainsbury's.

- Looking for cheaper petrol stations can save you money too, so long as you don't drive too far to get the better price.

- Other ways to save if things are really tight (in Lloyd's case) might be to try and reduce driving where possible and utilise an old bike to get to nearby places.

But please, know how to ride a bike before doing this- you'll end up with a dodgy knee and me and a whole lot of paperwork.

Necessities

At first, separating the "necessary" stuff from your needs can prove difficult, but it'll come down to your judgment call. It'll all be relative to you and your situation.

TOTAL	£1,821.93	AVERAGE	£607.31
Need	£694.47	Per Month	£231.49
Necessary	£155.79	Per Month	£51.93
Want	£712.14	Per Month	£237.38
OFWDIDT	£259.53	Per Month	£86.51

As for Lloyd, who spent **£51.93**, doing small things such as getting his haircut once every six weeks, instead of every four, could make a huge impact for him- and for you too!

Wants

Brace yourself, this might get painful. Reason being, this is usually where the worst leaks in your personal finances might be.

TOTAL	£1,821.93	AVERAGE	£607.31
Need	£694.47	Per Month	£231.49
Necessary	£155.79	Per Month	£51.93
Want	£712.14	Per Month	£237.38
OFWDIDT	£259.53	Per Month	£86.51

In Lloyd's case, he spent on average **£237.98** on his wants, that's greater than the amount that he spent on his needs!

And the truth is, like Lloyd, most of us are like this.

We spend more on the things we desire to have- the nice restaurant visits or the long holidays, than on the things we truly need.

Although this feels good in the moment, the end result is financially crippling.

For Lloyd, his weakness is his ability to spend a fortune on food and drink, outside of what he spends on his weekly grocery shop.

Yours could be anything, a Warhammer hobby, a few too many beers with the boys or maybe even a cigarette habit.

Perhaps it's your tendency to buy a ticket to every single concert you come across.

Or to change your phone every 18 months.

The list goes on and on...

But then, it's essential to strike a balance- just because you might not earn as much as you want doesn't imply that you should strip yourself entirely from the pleasures of life.

I mean, if you were on a journey in a desert and you had limited water, would you completely deprive yourself of drinking? No!

Instead, you would take little sips, cautioning your lips to restrain each time you held the bottle.

In the same likelihood, the goal isn't to stop attending to your cute little heart's desires; absolutely not.

Of course, if you do so, your own heart might turn against you (just kidding!).

But really, doing so can cause you to become de-motivated- and then, your efforts might seem useless.

You can strike the needed balance by allocating a certain percentage of your **debt-line** to spend on your wants, which should usually sit at about **50%**.

So, regardless of whatever amount you have left- whether great or small- you won't permit yourself to spend more than **50%** of whatever you have remaining after your bills are covered.

In times of need, i.e., you lose your job, your business goes bust, or you're struggling with a lot of high-interest debt, you may need to reduce this amount further (as Lloyd will be doing to the extreme, due to his situation), as it's important to be flexible.

Doing this might even further motivate you to earn more.

It's not being a tight arse like many of your friends might call it. It's called living within your means and anyone who doesn't will inevitably run into trouble.

OFWDIDT

Ah, this is possibly the easiest place to save money, because with a little more consideration, you never need to put money to waste.

Do this, and you won't need space for this in your semi-budget.

TOTAL	£1,821.93	AVERAGE	£607.31
Need	£694.47	Per Month	£231.49
Necessary	£155.79	Per Month	£51.93
Want	£712.14	Per Month	£237.38
OFWDIDT	£259.53	Per Month	£86.51

Now, before you judge ole Lloyd here, perhaps calculate yours first.

Mapping Out Your Semi-Budget

So, I know that my words could be likened to a spear for the last few pages. Pardon me for being so brutal.

That's now over and it's time to create your perfect semi-budget.

This can be recorded on the **My Spending Budget** table, which is also part of the **Monthly Expenditure Tab**.

To simplify things, let's see how Lloyd has created his budget, so you can do the same.

MY TOTAL SPENDING BUDGET	
My Debt Line	£400.37
Needs	£180.00
Necessary	
Wants	
Oh Dear	
TOTAL	£0.00
LEFT OVER	£400.37

In the past, Lloyd has been spending **£231.49** on average per month on his needs. But Lloyd's feeling brave and thinks that by implementing the techniques seen earlier, he can instead allocate just **£180** to cover these costs.

He won't know if he can until he tries, the worst thing that might happen is that he overshoots his budget a bit, but that's fine, odds are he will still be spending less than normal, and then he can adjust his budget accordingly.

Since he will be paying this every month regardless, Lloyd now adds his **Needs** budget to the list of his outgoings on the **Monthly Expenses Tab**.

Income	Amount	Monthly Expenses	Amount	Monthly Savings & Investments	Amount
Monthly Salary (Base Pay)	£1,693.55			My Pension Contribution	£84.67
Employer's Pension Contribution	£169.34			Employer's Pension Contribution	£169.34
		Tax	£112.28		
		National Insurance	£74.38		
		Worker's Union	£8.74		
		Rent Payment	£650.00		
		Council Tax	£80.99		
		Water	£22.21		
		Gas & Electric (Energy)	£72.92		
		Internet & TV	£26.99		
		Mobile Phone Bill	£10.00		
		Car Finance	£75.00		
		Sainsbury's Credit Card	£15.00		
		HSBC Credit Card	£60.00		
		Needs Budget	£180.00		
Total Income (Pre-Tax)	£1,862.89	Total Expenses (Pre-Tax)	£0.00	Total Savings/Investments (Pre-Tax)	£254.01
Total Income (Pre-Pay)	£1,608.88	Total Expenses (Pre-Pay)	£195.40	Total Savings/Investments (Pre-Pay)	£0.00
Total Income (Paid)	£1,413.48	Total Expenses (Paid)	£1,193.11	Total Savings/Investments (Paid)	£0.00

This way, his debt-line will decrease and become more accurate, as it truly represents how much he has to spend on himself and save after he has covered his cost of living.

MY TOTAL SPENDING BUDGET	
My Debt Line	£220.37
Needs	£180.00
Necessary	
Wants	
Oh Dear	
TOTAL	£0.00
LEFT OVER	£220.37

Now with **£220.37** remaining, he decides to allocate **£42** towards his necessities and **9.5%** of his remaining debt line on his wants (**£38.00**).

And as for his **OFWDIDT** expenses, he decides to take a little more care before every transaction, and with this new-found self-awareness, Lloyd realises there's no need to budget for this particular category.

MY TOTAL SPENDING BUDGET	
My Debt Line	£220.37
Needs	£180.00
Necessary	£42.00
Wants	£38.00
Oh Dear	£0.00
TOTAL	£80.00
LEFT OVER	£140.37

Lloyd now has a semi-budget that totals **£80.00**, to spend on himself, leaving him **£140.37** to start allocating towards paying off his outstanding debts and building up some savings.

Now that you've seen Lloyd's semi-budget, it's time to create yours. Good luck.

Your Maze Checklist:

Here's a summary of the steps outlined by Lloyd in this chapter, and as usual, you should probably get this done:

1. Look at your transactions for the last 90-days on your online banking history as your source of information, excluding those that you have already recorded on the **Monthly Expenses Tab**.

2. Record your findings in the **Monthly Expenditure Tab** using the amount and one of the four purpose categories. Ensure that you type the purpose name correctly, otherwise you may not get accurate figures.

3. Consider the sacrifices that you're willing to make. (Situation dependant of course).

4. Create your semi-budget for your **needs** first and then add that amount to your list of monthly expenses in the **Monthly Expenses Tab**.

5. Then use your new and improved **debt-line** to create the rest of your budget, whilst trying to leave as much left-over as possible.

6. Ensure your budget, excluding **Needs** is below your **debt-line**.

7. If it isn't, re-analyse your work. By trimming further and cutting even more stuff. Do all you can to get your budget under your maximum spending limit (**debt-line**).

8. Take a comfortable position on the chair where you are seated. And, with the most beautiful smile, appreciate how far you've come in your financial walk. (Most important step).

CHAPTER SEVEN

What To Do With All Your Extra Cash
Debts & How To Repay Them

Sincerely, we've now covered a whole lot.

In the previous chapter, you were courageous and believe me, I understand better than most just how tough some of the decisions that you might've made, may have been.

The decision to make sacrifices so that your finances can breathe again without life support will be the best one you've ever made.

But unfortunately, it might just take some time for you to realise.

However, now you've got all this extra cash, it raises the question.

What on earth should I do with it all?

Although using it to fund some ballroom dancing lessons may be nice, that's not quite the plan I've got in store for you.

"Alright then," you may be thinking, "Perhaps I'll pump it into a property business- or better still, buy some crypto coins?"

Fair try again, but no. Don't get me wrong- building up your investment portfolio adds a feather to your hat.

However, what's the point of becoming a modern-day Warren Buffet if you still have some outstanding bad debts to settle and/or don't have enough in a savings account to cover a large, unexpected expense?

I, more than most, prefer the riskier approaches to building wealth.

I know the only way that I'll continue to reach my ever-increasing wealth targets, is through taking risks, building a business, investing in crypto, that sort of thing.

However, that doesn't mean that I neglect the basics.

The way I see it, I can only follow that path if I have a solid foundation to fall back on, which is what we are working on now.

Repaying your debts- how do you do so?

Well, first of all you need to know the debts that you are currently in, the interest rates on those debts, and the minimum monthly repayments.

I do appreciate that you might not know all this off the top of your head, but with a mixture of running through any old paperwork, plus a few calls to any creditors, you should be able to get this information just fine.

Next, you will want to head to the **Debt Repayment Tab** on your Money Maze Spreadsheet, where you will find two tables.

In the first table, order your debts according to their interest rates- from the highest to the lowest.

In the second table, order your debts according to the amounts that you owe- this time from lowest to highest.

Remember that we are only recording our bad debts, mortgages & student loans can be forgotten about for now.

The Debt Avalanche			
Liabilities	Value	Interest	Minimum Payment
HSBC Credit Card	£3,000.00	21.10%	£60.00
Sainsbury's Credit Card	£700.00	18.90%	£15.00
Car Finance	£4,500.00	5.70%	£75.00
Total Liabilities	£8,200.00		

The Debt Snowball			
Liabilities	Value	Interest	Minimum Payment
Sainsbury's Credit Card	£700.00	18.90%	£15.00
HSBC Credit Card	£3,000.00	21.10%	£60.00
Car Finance	£4,500.00	5.70%	£75.00
Total Liabilities	£8,200.00		

Big thanks to Lloyd again for those amazing examples.

From there, there are two main ways to go about repaying your debts: either through the **debt avalanche** approach or the **debt snowball** approach.

Both means of debt repayment apply to most consumer debts: car finance, credit cards... you name it.

Both approaches are what people deep into the business world call **accelerated debt repayment plans**, as they help you to clear debt in a much quicker, more effective way.

However, both methods require you have some extra money earmarked to start overpaying.

This is precisely why I didn't talk about these plans back in Chapter I; I needed you to work your finances up to a point where you can have some extra money to spare- as that's the foundation on which these plans lie.

In both methods, you must make the **minimum payments** on all **debts** and then focus on targeting **one specific debt** with all that's left over.

Here's where these plans disagree. While the **debt avalanche** approach thinks you should divert the extra money towards the debt with the highest interest rate, the **debt snowball** approach believes that the smallest debt (in size) deserves the extra attention instead.

You'll get the final say in whose side you are on, but first, let me lay out the facts.

The Debt Avalanche Approach

This approach is mathematically great if you are laser-focused on clearing out the debts with the highest interest rates! This way, it leads to paying less interest in the long run.

While it is the best approach to saving money and time, it also has its downsides.

A major one is that it requires that you have a constant, fixed amount of extra cash each month- for the plan to work accurately, which also involves a lot of discipline.

So, it won't be particularly great for individuals who lose motivation quickly (simply skipping a month could disrupt the entire plan).

Lastly, this could be mentally taxing and hard to stick to.

The Debt Snowball Approach

In case you missed it, this is the method where the extra cash you have is driven into paying off your smaller debts first.

This approach focuses on one unique quality common amongst us all: being human.

Humans have feelings and emotions and are naturally wired to seek instant gratification.

When it comes to paying off debts, one way you can see it working quickly is to see them coming off your neck straight away.

These quick wins can really help you stay consistent.

Looking at this, this could be a huge advantage.

After all, the only way you can pay off your debt is if you consistently stick to the plan, and you can only stick to the plan if you feel good.

So, why not hop into a plan that makes you feel good and help you pay off your debts in the long run?

While that's great, this approach also has some downsides. For instance, you'll pay more in interest because of it.

Since you aren't paying off the debts with the highest interest rates first, you'll accumulate more debt as a result of these interests, leading to you having to pay more.

Let's see what Lloyd can do with his debts, so you may better understand what to do with yours.

This is still worth learning, even if you're debt-free, as you never know what may happen in the future.

Being prepared means that you can act quickly and be financially better off because of it.

First off, have it in mind that Lloyd factored in his minimum monthly payments back in Chapter 4 as part of his regular monthly expenses. (As you should have done as well).

So, the extra money he now has (**£140.37**) will be used to pay down one singular debt on top of the payment that he is already paying.

The Debt Avalanche

Liabilities	Value	Interest	Minimum Payment
HSBC Credit Card	£3,000.00	21.10%	£60.00
Sainsbury's Credit Card	£700.00	18.90%	£15.00
Car Finance	£4,500.00	5.70%	£75.00
Total Liabilities	**£8,200.00**		

If he were to opt for the debt avalanche approach, he'd allocate his left over **£140.37** into paying off his HSBC credit card first, chipping off a total of **£200.37** per month once combined with the payment of **£60** that he is already making.

Once paid off, he'd focus his efforts on credit card number 2, his Sainsbury's credit card, and finally, towards his car finance.

Once one debt topples, however, it free's up that minimum payment to start allocating towards the next debt too, meaning he'd be throwing **£215.37** at his Sainsbury's credit card and then **£290.37** towards his car finance.

If he stuck to this plan religiously, he'd be completely debt-free in 2 years and 6 months, paying **£1,206** in interest.

The Debt Snowball

Liabilities	Value	Interest	Minimum Payment
Sainsbury's Credit Card	£700.00	18.90%	£15.00
HSBC Credit Card	£3,000.00	21.10%	£60.00
Car Finance	£4,500.00	5.70%	£75.00
	Total Liabilities	£8,200.00	

But then, if he chose the debt snowball approach, he would first pour his money into his Sainsbury's credit card.

He'd then need to pounce on his HSBC credit card and, lastly, his car finance debt.

Here he would also be debt-free in 2 years and 6 months, this time paying **£1,229** in interest.

Which works out costing him **£23** more.

Look, I appreciate this might seem like a long time, but if you also throw any other money you earn, from bonuses/overtime and or gifts at these debts too, this can cut the time down considerably.

Nevertheless, your case could be way different from Lloyd's.

So, make sure you way the pros and cons of both approaches pertaining to your finances.

Then, choose a plan- and most importantly, stick to that plan! The bedrock of all of this is consistency.

There's no need to worry about the maths of all this either, as Lloyd used this calculator:

https://undebt.it/debt-snowball-calculator.php

How the calculator works

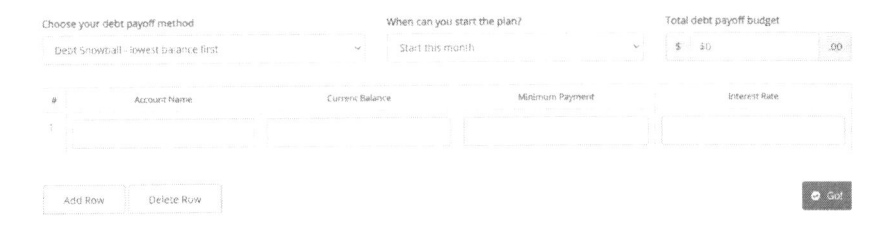

For each debt you have, add a new row- inputting its name, your current balance, the minimum payment required, along with its interest rate.

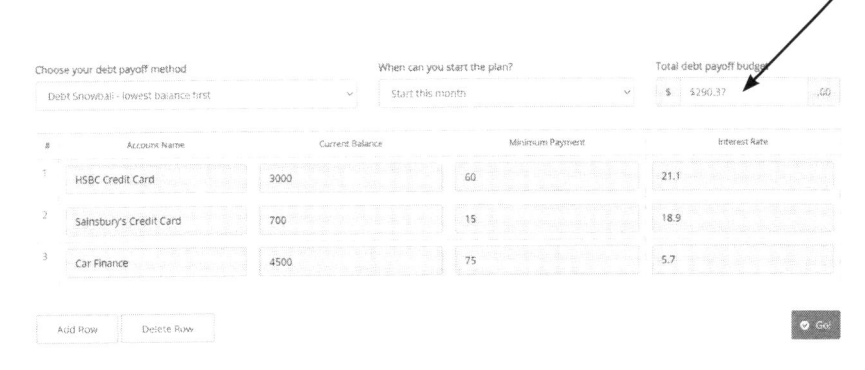

Towards the top-right of the calculator, you'll see a section called **total debt payoff budget**.

This means the total amount you can allocate towards paying off your debt- that is, the minimum payment for each debt, plus the extra cash you can afford.

For Lloyd, this is **£60** + **£75** + **£15** (His current minimum payments) + **£140.37** (The amount he has left after all spending has been accounted for) = **£290.37**

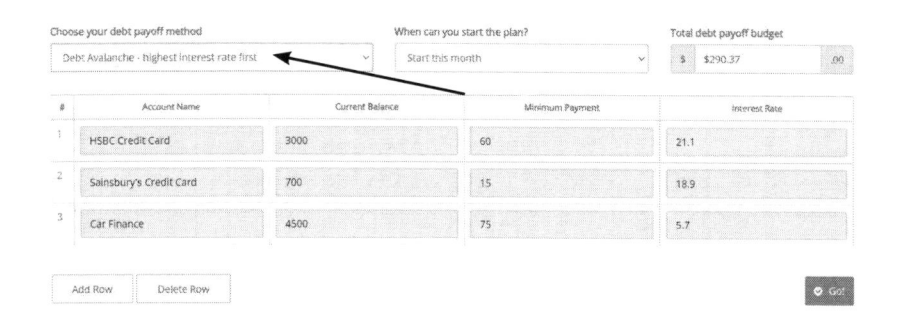

#	Account Name	Current Balance	Minimum Payment	Interest Rate
1	HSBC Credit Card	3000	60	21.1
2	Sainsbury's Credit Card	700	15	18.9
3	Car Finance	4500	75	5.7

Choose your debt payoff method: Debt Avalanche - highest interest rate first

When can you start the plan? Start this month

Total debt payoff budget: $290.37

Select the repayment method you are looking for in the top-left corner, whether the avalanche or snowball path. Then, click go!

By scrolling down to the bottom, you will be able to see how long it will take you to settle the debt and the interest you will pay.

Once the ball is rolling and your plans of freedom are set in place, it's worth staying away from using your credit cards/or taking out any additional debt, as it's like leaving your tap on while trying to save water.

Talking about credit cards, what if there was a way in which we could save money on the interest we need to pay back?

Getting the best deals on your credit card debts

There's no need to go into in-depth details about what a credit card is and its uses- you know it's those thin, rectangular pieces of plastic that allow you to spend the bank's money (in actual sense, borrow it).

And, since it is a form of debt, it attracts an annual percentage rate (APR).

Since most people find it challenging to pay off credit card debts banks have come up with an incentive that attracts new customers and helps them settle their credit card bills faster.

This is done in the form of a **balance transfer** product, which could potentially save you hundreds of pounds.

A credit card balance transfer involves moving outstanding debts from one credit card to another- usually from a credit card with a higher interest rate to one with a lower interest rate.

This new **balance transfer credit card** usually has a promotional interest rate of **0%**. However, this will only be for an introductory or promotional period (which could last from six to twelve months).

This comes at a one-off price- usually **3%** - **5%** of the transferred amount, which is generally lower than what you would have paid in interest anyway.

Although this sounds like heaven on earth, this route has some downsides- it requires diligence!

Carrying out a balance transfer still requires that you make an on-time payment each month of at least the minimum due of the transfer.

If you don't do so, you could lose the introductory period.

Again, before transferring your credit card balance, you must ensure that the regular interest rate you will be paying after the promotional period is less or equal to what you are presently paying.

If not, you might need to do another balance transfer when this offer ends if you won't have paid it off by then.

These offers can be found with a Google search- so put on your detective hat and go digging!

Understanding Car Debt

Before you skip this section because you aren't in any car debt, hold on.

Besides from credit cards, another kind of debt that usually holds us by the neck is car debt.

There are two primary reasons: first, who doesn't love cars?

Rather, who doesn't want to own a car? And secondly, cars often are depreciating assets.

So, with each passing year, they are less valuable than they previously were.

I'll explain a bit more so it can have a room in the VIP section of your brain.

On average, a new car loses **20%** of its initial value every year. So, by the third year, its residual value will have dropped to just **40%** of the price you paid.

Of course, since we are talking in percentages, the value decline due to depreciation is steeper if you compare luxury, expensive cars that could cost as much as **£40,000** to smaller, cheaper cars.

Something that has helped me when dealing with cars is to not buy any car that is worth more than **20%** of my yearly income, which means when I eventually do buy one, I can do so outrightly.

This rule works well as it prevents the need for having to get a finance agreement, as the price range of the car will be within my capacity to save and purchase outright.

If you're like Lloyd and have taken out a car finance or were thinking about it, I'll explain a bit more about how it works.

You can buy a car through one of two agreements: the first being a **hire purchase** (**HP**) and the second being a **personal contract purchase** (**PCP**).

In a **HP** plan, the car's price is broken down into an initial deposit and then a series of monthly payments.

And by the end of the term, you'll own the car outright.

When entering a **PCP** plan, the initial cost of the car is also divided into an initial deposit and consecutive monthly payments.

A significant difference between **PCP** and **HP** is that if you want to own the car, you have to pay a lump sum- known as a **balloon payment**- at the end of the agreed period.

However, the monthly payments will be lower than what you would have paid in an **HP** plan.

If you're dead set on getting out of car debt before the term is up, you may be charged an early exit fee, so it is worth double-checking what this may be.

There is also the option of leasing a car, of course.

You won't have to worry about depreciation or balloon payments- just ensure you keep up with your monthly payments, just like renting a house!

This means you'll get the latest model at a much cheaper rate than if you were to finance the car but are tied into a lengthy agreement that can eat away at you every month.

You've also got to be very careful when showing off- you don't want to damage it!

Stuck in other types of debts?

Aside from credit cards and car debts, there are many other borrowing options out there,

The most common being personal loans and overdrafts.

Personal Loans

There are two main kinds of debts in the financial world- **secured debts** and **unsecured debts**.

Secured debts require that you back up your loan request with collateral- for instance, a house or a car- which the bank can liquidate if you fail to pay off the loan at a stated time.

On the other hand, **unsecured debts** do not require collateral but usually require a high credit score. (Which I'll speak more on shortly).

Personal loans usually have a fixed interest rate for the loan timeframe; hence, your repayment will be fixed each month.

The best way to repay personal loans is to do so quickly, by overpaying.

Most lenders will allow you to pay back in full before the end of the term. However, you might need to pay a charge, typically around one to two months' interest for the privilege.

Overdrafts

An **overdraft** is another form of highly costly borrowing as it allows you to use more money that is actually in your current account and can be especially expensive if you do so without giving your bank prior notice.

An **authorised overdraft** has to be arranged with your bank and will allow you to borrow a certain amount up to a limit, which is usually cheaper.

An **unauthorised overdraft** is where you spend more than is actually in your current account, without letting your bank know beforehand.

This can be very costly, with high interest rates and penalty charges.

Similar to a **0%** balance transfer card, you can get out of an expensive overdraft through the use of a long-term **money transfer card**.

A money transfer card allows you, with a fee, to transfer an amount into your account that can then be repaid every month at a **0%** interest rate for a set period of time.

Credit Scores

The trouble with these money saving techniques, is that it all depends on having a good credit score, which if you are in debt quite badly, might not be very good at all.

Hence, the better your credit score, the higher the chances of being approved for a loan.

All a **credit score** is, is a three-digit number that financial agencies calculate based of your past borrowing habits.

Simply put- the more you repay on time, the higher your score.

When a company searches for your credit score, the process is known as a **credit check**.

Credit checks help financial companies determine your financial behaviour before handing you out money.

These checks come in the form of **soft credit checks** and **hard credit checks**.

The main difference between these two is that soft credit checks do not leave footprints on your credit report, whilst hard checks leave visible evidence.

Too much evidence, could imply to lenders that you are struggling financially.

This includes things such as taking out a phone contract, applying for a mortgage and, of course, applying for a personal loan.

Before applying to any of these, you must be sure that your chances of getting your application approved are high- and this is where soft checks come in.

Whenever you search for your own credit score or use an online credit-score checker, you are carrying out a soft check. Luckily, soft checks don't leave traces on your report, so they are helpful in the determination of your eligibility rating.

Also, note that a soft check can also be carried out whenever a company searches your credit report as part of an identity check.

You can check your credit score via several online credit report companies, one being Experian:

https://www.experian.co.uk/consumer/experian-credit-score.html

The best way to get loans at the cheapest rates is to have a good credit score, and a sure-fire way of having an excellent credit score is repaying whatever you borrow, whenever it's due.

If you're into those serial killer documentaries on Netflix, then the worst way to murder your credit score is from obtaining a **payday loan**.

In case you don't know, **payday loans** are high-rate, short-term loans designed to keep you afloat until the end of the month.

The money is paid directly into your account- and you must repay the borrowed amount alongside the extremely high interest.

If you are really strapped for cash, there are other options that should be considered first, like selling some of your old stuff on Facebook marketplace or eBay, before even thinking about a payday loan.

Student Loans

Earlier in this book, I asked you not to record your student loans on your list of liabilities, and here's why:

Student loans are more like taxes; taxes you only begin to repay after your income crosses a particular threshold.

Again, just like taxes, if your income goes below the threshold or you stop working, you are exempted from paying the student loan.

This threshold is determined by the repayment plan you might currently be on.

There are four types of repayment plans: Plan 1, Plan 2, Plan 4, and Postgraduate loans.

If you've got a student loan, then you can head over to:

https://www.gov.uk/sign-in-to-manage-your-student-loan-balance

to determine the repayment plan that you are on.

- Plan 1 – If your income is over **£19,895** per year.

- Plan 2- If your income is over **£27,295** per year.

- Plan 4 – If your income is over **£25,000** per year.

- Postgraduate loan - If your income is over **£21,000** per year.

The actual amount you repay is **9%** above your threshold if you fall under Plans 1, 2, and 4 - and **6%** above your threshold if you've also got a postgraduate loan.

For instance, if Lloyd earned **£30,000** per year and falls under plan 2, he'd have to pay **9%** of the difference between his earnings and his plan's threshold.

£30,000 - £27,295 = £2,705

9% of £2,705 = £243.45

Therefore, this will end up costing Lloyd roughly £20 per month.

£243.45 ÷ 12 = £20.29

In summary…

I should hope that we can all now agree on one thing: settling debts isn't impossible, although, yes, it will take time and energy.

While getting out of debt is great, we need to look beyond that; our next goal should be to make sure that we don't ever end up in that position again, which I will be covering in the next chapter.

To which I'm sure some of you non in debt people are looking forward to.

It might be worth using this period of financial constraint to train yourself to live within your means so that when you are finally out of the storms, you won't find yourself running back to old ways.

Lastly, if you still find yourself stuck in so much debt that you feel being debt-free is an impossibility:

Seek professional advice.

There are organisations that can help you, such as the **Citizen's Advice Bureau**.

You'll be able to speak with a trained financial advisor, who will offer you personalised guidance about debts and the exact steps that you should take.

Here's the link to contact them:

https://www.citizensadvice.org.uk/debt-and-money/

Your Maze Checklist

That's pretty much all we have to cover in this chapter. This homework applies to anyone carrying debt; for those of you who aren't, enjoy your break.

1. Gather the information you need and fill out both tables in the **Debt Repayment Tab**.

2. Check for any hidden fees. You will find all of these details in your paperwork. If you can't find that, contact your lender immediately.

3. Apply debt savings techniques.

Do research to know if you could get better deals on your debt and the interest you are paying.

If you hit the jackpot, re-do the table, taking account of the new deal you just bagged.

4. Using the calculator, calculate what you will have to pay using each debt settlement approach. Which of these ways do you consider best for you- and your pocket?

Decide which path to follow.

5. Once you pick an approach, adjust your monthly expenses in the Monthly Expenses Tab to reflect the changes to your debt payments. (Easily forgotten).

6. Then, if you haven't already, go about adjusting your debt repayments by reducing them all down to their minimum payment, bar the debt you are going to target first, and put your remaining money towards that.

The Money Maze

Income	Amount	Monthly Expenses	Amount	Monthly Savings & Investments	Amount
Monthly Salary (Base Pay)	£1,693.55			My Pension Contribution	£84.67
Employer's Pension Contribution	£169.34			Employer's Pension Contribution	£169.34
		Tax	£112.28		
		National Insurance	£74.38		
		Worker's Union	£8.74		
		Rent Payment	£650.00		
		Council Tax	£80.99		
		Water	£22.21		
		Gas & Electric (Energy)	£72.92		
		Internet & TV	£26.99		
		Mobile Phone Bill	£10.00		
		Car Finance	£75.00		
		Sainsbury's Credit Card	£15.00		
		HSBC Credit Card	£200.37		
		Needs Budget	£180.00		
Total Income (Pre-Tax)	£1,862.89	Total Expenses (Pre-Tax)	£0.00	Total Savings/Investments (Pre-Tax)	£254.01
Total Income (Pre-Pay)	£1,608.88	Total Expenses (Pre-Pay)	£195.40	Total Savings/Investments (Pre-Pay)	£0.00
Total Income (Paid)	£1,413.48	Total Expenses (Paid)	£1,333.48	Total Savings/Investments (Paid)	£0.00

CHAPTER EIGHT

How & Where To Save
Let's Talk About Accounts

I'm hoping that you're smiling right now; I should like to think that things are now looking better than before, no matter your personal situation.

Remember what I said in the introduction- if you don't get any results, there's a refund waiting for you.

For those of you who have results, what should you do once your debt free?

The constraints you will experience when trying to settle debt shouldn't be treated as a just a sacrifice.

It's part of your financial journey and so when you introduce this to everyday life, you'll find it easier to save more, and when you do so, you will become indoctrinated into this financial principle- saving.

Having some savings not only brings peace of mind for rainy days but can also be a great source of motivation.

Watching that pile grow bigger and bigger is quite the feeling, if you're anything like me that is.

Where should you save?

The best place to save is usually a **savings account**, which I am sure many of you may already have.

Your money is safe, and the probability that the bank will lose your money is close to none (except if what happens during the opening scene of the Dark Night occurs).

Throughout this book, I have referenced **interest**, mainly in the terms of what we have to pay.

However, this time when I speak about interest, I am talking about the money that we earn, again is usually being expressed in the form of an **Annual Percentage Rate (APR)**.

The higher the interest rate, the more we get paid.

But then, unfortunately, interest rates are at an all-time low. So, although this makes borrowing cheaper, you don't get to make much on what you do have.

The interest rate is determined by the Bank of England- through their **base rate** (also known as the **bank rate**).

The base rate is the interest rate the Bank of England offers to commercial banks for either holding money with them or borrowing.

So, the interest rates these commercial banks offer you is affected by the base rate the Bank of England gives them.

Asides from affecting the interest rate, the Bank of England also fights against **inflation**. Something you may have heard quite a lot about in 2022.

Inflation refers to the gradual decrease in the purchasing power that a sum of money has.

The root cause of inflation is the increased supply of money. Look at it this way: whenever you have lots of your favourite drink at home, you don't usually value it- you can easily share it with your friends and family.

However, its value increases when you don't have much of it. So, likewise, when there isn't so much money in circulation, the value of money is heightened.

But, when the money in circulation increases, the value of money is reduced- and so is its purchasing power.

So, the Bank of England controls the amount of money let out into the economy and tries to keep inflation at bay.

The inflation rate typically rises every year regardless. With a coordinated effort from the Bank of England, inflation can usually be kept below 2% per year.

Simply put: If you had **£100** and inflation is at **2%**, the following year, in reality, your **£100** would only be able to purchase **£98** worth of goods.

Inflation at its peak can be very dangerous for an economy. Here, the currency of the country rapidly loses its value.

This is known as **hyperinflation**. For example, in Zimbabwe, a country in Africa. At some point in their history, inflation hit about 230,000,000 percent- making their currency essentially worthless.

So worthless that in actual fact there were 100 trillion Zimbabwe Dollar bills in circulation. Yeah... that's bad!

While inflation might sound like a terrible financial concept, a small, controlled amount of it each year is seen as a good thing.

This is because inflation encourages buyers to spend- thereby increasing the demands for goods and keeping businesses profitable.

Some might argue that the best way to curb inflation is to allow for **deflation**.

Deflation refers to the increase in the purchasing power of money over time.

While this argument might seem logical, you should understand that with an increased value of a currency comes the decreased profitability of businesses- as the demand for goods and services is reduced.

So, rather than stopping it entirely, let's just keep inflation in check and let nature do its thing.

Why is this important to you?

Although savings can be a great use of your money, inflation can be a massive downside.

If the bank offers an interest rate of **0.1%**- and inflation is at **2%**- you're losing roughly **1.9%** of your money's value, year over year.

Nevertheless, a massive advantage of cash savings is that it is a liquid asset.

For instance, if you had a car breakdown, you could easily dip your hands into your savings rather than relying on a credit card.

Financial experts usually suggest that your goal should be having at least three months' worth of regular monthly expenses saved up in an emergency fund.

Once you've achieved this, depending on your risk tolerance, you can perhaps start taking other steps with your money, such as investing or increasing your emergency fund to six months.

For Lloyd, this will mean that his first savings target should be:

£1,193.11 x 3 = £3,605.55

This is why you must find a bank that offers a reasonable interest rate on your savings account- as a way to combat the menace of inflation.

There are many different banks with various accounts, so which one should you choose?

The short answer- it all depends.

Easy-Access Savings Accounts

As the name implies, an easy-access savings account offers you flexibility while still presenting competitive interest rates.

Unlike other types of savings' accounts, which have many restrictions and conditions, easy access accounts are simple to set up and manage.

In addition, you don't have to offer any substantial deposit when opening the account, making it the perfect place for newbies to begin saving.

Easy-access savings accounts are particularly good if you are saving for an emergency fund, as your money can be retrieved at a moment's notice.

A downside to this kind of account is that you will usually find that they offer low interest rates, as a price for flexibility.

Before choosing a bank, ensure you compare across the board (I'm sure you are familiar with this rule).

Luckily, the money savings expert can help us with that, with their brilliant website:

https://www.moneysavingexpert.com/savings/savings-accounts-best-interest/

Easy-access accounts – what we'd go for

Cynergy Bank currently pays the top easy-access rate of 0.66%. Its account allows unlimited withdrawals and can be opened online with £1. However, the rate plummets to just 0.3% after a year, so diarise for then to check for better options.

Or, if you prefer a high-street banking name, Nationwide pays 0.45%, though it only allows three penalty-free withdrawals per year and will give you a lower rate after a year.

MSE Analysis

Provider	Rate (AER variable)	Unlimited withdrawals?	Min/max deposit	How to open	Max FSCS protection
Top standard easy-access rates. Here are the highest paying traditional accounts.					
Cynergy Bank	0.66% (1)	✓	£1/ £1m	Online	£85,000
Shawbrook Bank	0.62%	✓ (2)	£1,000/ £85,000	Online	£85,000
Marcus*	0.6% (3)	✓	£1/ £250,000	Online	£85,000 (4)
Top high-street savings account. The rate's lower but we know many prefer saving with a big name.					
Nationwide*	0.45%	✗ (3/yr) (5)	None/ £5m	Online/ app	£85,000
Easy-access savings via other routes (click links to read more)					
Virgin Money current account	2.02%	✓	None/ £1,000	Online	£85,000, shared (6)
Nationwide current account	2%	✓	None/ £1,500	Online	£85,000

Looking at this table, the bank currently offering the best rate is **Cynergy Bank** at **0.66%**.

This particular account can be opened with as low as **£1**, you are also qualified for unlimited withdrawals and a maximum deposit of **£1,000,000**.

In addition to this, it is also covered under the **financial services compensation scheme**, meaning that should the bank ever go bust, you will be entitled to retrieving your money back, all the way up to **£85,000**.

Please check out the website for yourself, as it is constantly being updated, so please don't go off these examples!

The chances are, another bank may have already taken the top spot, and we don't want to go missing out on good deals now do we?

Some of the best rates only last for as long as a year, and so, it is a good idea to be on the lookout for better deals, even after opening your account.

If Lloyd was to place his **£3,605.55** in here, he could expect to be paid **£23.80** in interest.

Meaning, that if inflation was at **2%**, his savings would decrease in purchasing power by **1.44%**.

Take a breath.

Notice Savings Accounts

If you think you need some kind of disciplinary measure when saving, check this out.

Notice savings accounts involve a waiting period whenever you want to use the money you've tucked away.

Instead of getting access to your cash immediately, you must give an advanced directive to the bank weeks, or even months before you want to access your money.

The waiting period could range from as low as 32 days to as high as 120 days.

This initiative may help keep your spending urges at bay. Plus, you can typically access a higher interest rate- so it's a double win!

This time, still use the money saving expert's website, but select notice savings accounts.

Provider	Rate (AER variable)	Notice	Min/max deposit	How to open	Max FSCS protection
OakNorth Bank	1.06%	120 days	£1/ £500,000	Online/ app (1)	£85,000
Close Brothers	1.05%	95 days	£10,000/ £2m	Online	£85,000
Secure Trust Bank (2)	0.85%	60 days	£1,000/ £1m	Online	£85,000
Investec via Raisin (3)	0.8% + £50 bonus for some	32 days	£1,000/ £85,000	Online	£85,000

(1) Joint accounts can only be opened online. (2) Maximum of 4 interest withdrawals and 3 capital withdrawals per year. (3) Can't be opened as a joint account.

According to this data set, **OakNorth Bank** is offering the best interest rate at **1.06%**. However, you'll notice (pardon the pun) that you'll have to give them 120 days warning before accessing your money!

Notice savings accounts tend to be best if you know in advance when you want to use the money; for instance, saving for a holiday that is 2 years away.

If you wanted to have a shorter notice period instead, then looking at this same table, **Investec via Raisin** offers only a 32-day notice period.

This might be better suited for saving for Christmas or a birthday.

Fixed Savings Accounts

Regarding getting the best interest rates, fixed savings accounts are the kings! Unfortunately, they also come with their terms and conditions.

Like a notice savings account, there timeframe is attached to when you can access your savings.

Difference is, instead of giving the bank a heads-up, your money is totally locked away until the term is up.

Unlike a notice savings account, you cannot add to the initial deposit you make when opening the account.

This tends to make this better suited for perhaps if you ever come into a large sum of money and need some time to think about what to do with it.

There are a variety of fixes out there- one, two, three, four, and even five-years.

The longer you are separated from your money, the higher the interest rates.

It also goes without saying that you can find more about these accounts on the same website we have already been using above.

Regular Savings Accounts

Although these accounts offer great rates compared to the traditional fixed or easy-access savings accounts, you will have to fulfil some strict terms and conditions in order to access all the benefits.

For instance, you may need to have another product with the same bank- usually a current account.

Some other hurdles you might have to deal with; include having a limited number of withdrawals or having to make a deposit every month.

On the brighter side, when you pass the criteria and agree to the terms of this account, you could be eligible to receive some great rates!

Individual Savings Accounts

An Individual Savings Account (ISAs) is a type of savings account that allows you to either invest or save tax-free.

There are five different types of ISA products, namely:

- Cash ISAs
- Stock & Shares ISAs
- Innovative Finance ISAs
- Lifetime ISAs
- Junior ISAs

Each of these has its respective purpose, and you are eligible to have up to **£20,000** in your ISAs each tax year- meaning you can spread this across all five accounts (which can be opened at most building societies and banks across the UK).

Note that you cannot pay into more than one kind of ISA (for instance, you cannot have more than one Cash ISA each year), and other restrictions may apply to some particular ISA's.

When you put your money into an ISA, you do not pay tax on the capital gains (yes, another form of tax) from the investments or the interests from the accounts.

Whereas usually on you'd have to pay tax on anything you earn over **£1,000** for the basic tax rate and **£500** on the higher tax rate.

Cash ISAs are very beneficial when you have access to a high-interest rate. This is because you will reach the tax-free allowance faster so that the tax break you receive can come in handy.

Stocks & Shares ISAs provide you with capital gains (as long as your investments go well).

When an investment asset is sold, the profit from the sale is referred to as **capital gains**.

Typically, tax applies to these gains. However, with this kind of ISA, your profits are tax-free, up to **£20,000**.

What you will notice however, is that I will not be covering investments as such in this book, as sometimes it can be tempting to skip the foundational steps, we have already covered to pursue some excitement, so that we don't feel that we are missing out on the market.

We will cover that in a future book, but for now, let's make sure we build this base, get out of debt, and have a solid emergency fund first.

Lifetime ISAs, offer a way to either save for later in life or to buy your first home. Every year, you can deposit as much as **£4,000** into this account and get a **25%** bonus from the government on your savings.

Aside from your employer's pension, this is another way to get free money.

However, you must be above 18 and below 40 to be able to get this bonus.

You can also only withdraw from this account if you are about to purchase your first home (below **£450,000**), or you are 60 and over and/or are terminally ill with less than 12 months to live.

If you do not meet these conditions and still intend to withdraw, you will have to pay a **25%** withdrawal fee (which essentially just takes back the bonus).

Innovative Finance ISAs can also be classified as some sort of investment. This is because it involves two people: one who needs a loan and another willing to lend.

This kind of ISA allows you to engage in peer-to-peer loans to earn a higher interest on your cash, as you will be the one lending.

This does involve risk and so therefore can be seen as a type of investing.

However, in 2019, the Financial Conduct Authority (FCA) imposed stricter rules to protect less experienced lenders, so that the risk levels are lower.

Since you will be cutting out the bank, the chances of obtaining a higher interest rate are good.

Junior ISAs, help you ensure your child's future.

If your child is below 18 and lives in the UK, they are qualified for this kind of account.

If your child lives outside the UK however, you must fulfil two criteria: firstly, you must be a Crown servant, and secondly, your child must depend on you for care.

You can either open a Cash Junior ISA- wherein you don't pay any tax on the interest received from the money saved.

Or you can open a Junior Stocks & Shares- where you don't pay tax on the capital gains made.

You can put in a maximum of **£9,000** each tax year- and the total amount in the account can be accessible to them once they are 18.

Luckily for you, there's no homework in this chapter. Instead, we will be covering how to implement what we have just learnt in the next; almost there!

CHAPTER NINE

How To Organise Your Finances
Different Accounts, Tracking Net Worth & Automation

The good news is that the death by information bit is now done.

It's time to finalise everything we've learned and create a system that makes your money work for you.

This is what I mean: I'm pretty sure you've got a current account and a savings account.

Maybe you just opened these accounts or stumbled across them as a teenager.

However, if you don't create a system of how (and when) you should move your money each month, it leaves room for error.

Nothing is more nerve-racking than looking at your bank account and not knowing what bills are yet to come out and in turn how much you have left to blow on a night out.

Some might say- "Make all your bills come out on the first of every month".

My argument is, what if this happens to be a Saturday? And you get paid on the last working day; you'll be going that whole weekend not having a clue what you can spend.

What I want to do in this chapter (as I round off) is help you create a functional system of moving your money around in the easiest, most effortless, and straightforward way possible.

Ready?

The solution is...

Multiple accounts.

Here's how it works: You'll need to separate your money into three distinct accounts: a master account, a spending account, and a savings account.

These three accounts make up the three pillars of the personal-finance foundation that I have been referring to throughout this book.

Let's begin with the master account.

Master (Bills) Account

Your master, also known as your bills account, is where all your money (from your income sources) should come in and where all your bills (monthly expenses) should go out.

The idea is that you will be paid your monthly salary on your payday in this account, and from there you can move your money about.

Note- it might be worth leaving a buffer amount- perhaps **£100**, in this account at all times. This way, you're protected if you get a larger-than-expected bill.

Spending Account

The spending account is where the semi-budget approach is taken into full effect.

Allocating your spending budget (made in chapter six) to a secondary current account paints the clearest possible picture of what you are and aren't able to spend.

It doesn't matter who you go with, but it's usually easier to go with a different bank, as it saves getting your two cards mixed up.

No more uncertainty about if you can afford that new Nike shoe or the shirt that caught your fancy across town; your account balance tells you vividly.

This type of budgeting works as you can view your spending patterns as a whole rather than in isolated categories.

In some cases, you can be sure that if you get that shirt, you just sacrificed getting your next haircut.

Savings (Emergency Funds) Account

The final account that you'll need is a savings account, primarily to save up your emergency fund.

Here you can put any leftover money after your budget, bills and that you haven't allocated towards spending until you reach your goal.

Any regular savings that you are planning to make should then be recorded in **Red Section** of the **Monthly Savings & Investments Column** of the **Monthly Expenses Tab** of your spreadsheet.

Income	Amount	Monthly Expenses	Amount	Monthly Savings & Investments	Amount
Monthly Salary (Base Pay)	£1,693.55			My Pension Contribution	£84.67
Employer's Pension Contribution	£169.34			Employer's Pension Contribution	£169.34
		Tax	£112.28		
		National Insurance	£74.38		
		Worker's Union	£8.74		
		Rent Payment	£650.00	Emergency Fund	£0.00
		Council Tax	£80.99		
		Water	£22.21		
		Gas & Electric (Energy)	£72.92		
		Internet & TV	£26.99		
		Mobile Phone Bill	£10.00		
		Car Finance	£75.00		
		Sainsbury's Credit Card	£15.00		
		HSBC Credit Card	£200.37		
		Needs Budget	£180.00		
Total Income (Pre-Tax)	£1,862.89	Total Expenses (Pre-Tax)	£0.00	Total Savings/Investments (Pre-Tax)	£254.01
Total Income (Pre-Pay)	£1,608.88	Total Expenses (Pre-Pay)	£195.40	Total Savings/Investments (Pre-Pay)	£0.00
Total Income (Paid)	£1,413.48	Total Expenses (Paid)	£1,333.48	Total Savings/Investments (Paid)	£0.00

For Lloyd however, anything he can he is putting towards repaying his debts first, before building up his emergency fund.

Interest rates matter here and so pick carefully but remember to make sure you can access that money should you need to, without too many hiccups.

And that's it; the three pillars are complete.

Do you need any other accounts?

After you've paid off your debts and filled up your emergency funds to the very brim you can then choose to extend your reach into other accounts.

For instance, you might want to open a Lifetime ISA if you intend to own a home a couple of years from now, or perhaps open a particular account for Christmas or to fund a holiday.

Personally, I love to have not more than 5 accounts holding cash - a master account, a spending account, an emergency funds account, a specific one-off savings account, and perhaps, a joint account.

Let's briefly discuss those:

Joint accounts- do you need them?

If you have a partner, then this is worth considering.

A benefit of joint accounts is that it helps you- and your partner- contribute towards paying your shared bills, such as the mortgage, rent, groceries, energy, you name it...

It's not for me to intrude and tell you how much to pay towards any shared bills you may have.

What I will do however, is tell you how I do it and you can sit down and have a discussion with your partner or roommate/s as to how you want to go about doing it.

My long-term girlfriend and I split our expenses based on the ratio of our earnings. For example, if I hypothetically earned **65%** of our combined household income, then I would pay **65%** towards the total of our shared monthly expenses into the joint account.

She would then contribute the remaining **35%** and that money can cover our shared bills, whilst also leaving a nice **£100** float again.

Won't you get confused with so many accounts?

If that is on your mind, you aren't alone.

While coming up with this strategy, this was also on my mind.

However, I created a means that keeps confusion as far away as possible.

A common reason many people are reluctant to arrange their finances in this manner is that they would prefer seeing all their money at one glance rather than having it distributed across many accounts.

And really, that's a fair point.

So, I added this feature to the money maze spreadsheet; you can log all the details of all your different accounts and assets, giving you the place to view your whole financial picture.

If you take a trip to the **Accounts Tab**, you'll see what I'm on about.

Showing that it is in fact possible to separate your money into different accounts and still benefit from viewing it all in one place.

Amazing, right?

Spending Accounts	Value	Liabilities	Value	Saving Accounts & Assets	Value	Investing Accounts	Value
Current Accounts	£	"Good" Debt	£	Savings Accounts	£	Pensions	£
Credit Cards (Useful)	£	"Bad Debt"	£	Assets	£	Businesses	£
Savings (Bills/Spendable)	£			Debtors	£	Investments	£

Spendable Income	£0.00
Liabilities	£0.00
Savings, Assets & Debtors	£0.00
Investments	£0.00
Net Wealth	£0.00

As you can see, the page is broken down into four primary columns- **Spending Accounts**, **Liabilities**, **Savings & Assets**, and **Investing Accounts**- which are further divided into different categories.

Let's begin from the left-hand side: the **Spending Column**.

Once you've opened the necessary accounts you want to use, log the values of your master account, spending account, and joint accounts (if you have one) in the **Current Accounts Sub-Heading**.

Spending Accounts	Value	Liabilities	Value	Saving Accounts & Assets	Value	Investing Accounts	Value
Current Accounts	£	"Good" Debt	£	Savings Accounts	£	Pensions	£
Barclay's Current Account	£100.00						
Monzo Spending Account	£80.00						
Credit Cards (Useful)	£	"Bad Debt"	£	Assets	£	Businesses	£
Savings (Bills/Spendable)	£			Debtors	£	Investments	£

Spendable Income	£180.00
Liabilities	£0.00
Savings, Assets & Debtors	£0.00
Investments	£0.00
Net Wealth	£180.00

You'll notice that Lloyd has logged his most regular values in each of these accounts.

That being his **£100** buffer for his master account and the regular **£80** that he has budgeted for his spending account.

He's done this because the amounts in these accounts will constantly be changing, therefore saving making changes all the time.

Skip the **Credit Card Category** for now, as later on, I'll show you how you can use credit cards within your budget.

Now list the values of any specific savings accounts you have that you are intending to spend, i.e., a Christmas fund, in the **Savings (Bills/Spendable) Section**. (Should you have or want any).

Spending Accounts	Value	Liabilities	Value	Saving Accounts & Assets	Value	Investing Accounts	Value
Current Accounts	£	"Good" Debt	£	Savings Accounts	£	Pensions	£
Barclay's Current Account	£100.00						
Monzo Spending Account	£80.00						
Credit Cards (Useful)	£	"Bad Debt"	£	Assets	£	Businesses	£
Savings (Bills/Spendable)	£			Debtors	£	Investments	£
Christmas/Birthday's Fund	£0.00						
Yearly Expenses Fund	£0.00						
Spendable Income	£180.00						
Liabilities	£0.00						
Savings, Assets & Debtors	£0.00						
Investments	£0.00						
Net Wealth	£180.00						

This section is for savings that you are intending on spending anyway and so don't include your emergency fund here.

You'll now know your **Spendable Income**:

Spendable Income	£180.00
Liabilities	£0.00
Savings, Assets & Debtors	£0.00
Investments	£0.00

Net Wealth	£180.00

Next, hop to the **Liabilities Column**. Do you have any good debts or bad debts? Include whatever debts you have here from your **Initial Wealth Tab**.

Spending Accounts	Value	Liabilities	Value	Saving Accounts & Assets	Value	Investing Accounts	Value
Current Accounts	£	"Good" Debt	£	Savings Accounts	£	Pensions	£
Barclay's Current Account	£100.00						
Monzo Spending Account	£80.00						
Credit Cards (Useful)	£	"Bad Debt"	£	Assets	£	Businesses	£
		Sainsbury's Credit	£700.00				
		HSBC Credit Card	£3,000.00				
		Car Finance	£4,500.00				
Savings (Bills/Spendable)	£			Debtors	£	Investments	£
Christmas/Birthday's Fund	£0.00						
Yearly Expenses Fund	£0.00						

Spendable Income	£180.00
Liabilities	£8,200.00
Savings, Assets & Debtors	£0.00
Investments	£0.00
Net Wealth	-£8,020.00

Then, go to the **Savings & Assets Column**. Under the **Savings Category**, here you can input your emergency fund and any other long-term savings account, such as a Lifetime ISA.

Spending Accounts	Value	Liabilities	Value	Saving Accounts & Assets	Value	Investing Accounts	Value
Current Accounts	£	"Good" Debt	£	Savings Accounts	£	Pensions	£
Barclay's Current Account	£100.00			Cynergy Bank Emergency Fund	£50.00		
Monzo Spending Account	£80.00						
Credit Cards (Useful)	£	"Bad Debt"	£	Assets	£	Businesses	£
		Sainsbury's Credit	£700.00				
		HSBC Credit Card	£3,000.00				
		Car Finance	£4,500.00				
Savings (Bills/Spendable)	£			Debtors	£	Investments	£
Christmas/Birthday's Fund	£0.00						
Yearly Expenses Fund	£0.00						

Spendable Income	£180.00
Liabilities	£8,200.00
Savings, Assets & Debtors	£50.00
Investments	£0.00
Net Wealth	-£7,970.00

Then, under the **Assets Category**, head back to the **Initial Wealth Tab** on your spreadsheet, copy any other assets you have listed there and add it to this section.

Spending Accounts	Value	Liabilities	Value	Saving Accounts & Assets	Value	Investing Accounts	Value
Current Accounts	£	"Good" Debt	£	Savings Accounts	£	Pensions	£
Barclay's Current Account	£100.00			Cynergy Bank Emergency Fund	£50.00		
Monzo Spending Account	£80.00						
Credit Cards (Useful)	£	"Bad Debt"	£	Assets	£	Businesses	£
		Sainsbury's Credit	£700.00	Vauxhall Corsa	£4,000.00		
		HSBC Credit Card	£3,000.00				
		Car Finance	£4,500.00				
Savings (Bills/Spendable)	£			Debtors	£	Investments	£
Christmas/Birthday's Fund	£0.00						
Yearly Expenses Fund	£0.00						

Spendable Income	£180.00
Liabilities	£8,200.00
Savings, Assets & Debtors	£4,050.00
Investments	£0.00
Net Wealth	-£3,970.00

You can also impact any debtors. For instance, are you owed any money from someone, a friend, or a company?

Here's the place to input that too.

Spending Accounts	Value	Liabilities	Value	Saving Accounts & Assets	Value	Investing Accounts	Value
Current Accounts	£	"Good" Debt	£	Savings Accounts	£	Pensions	£
Barclay's Current Account	£100.00			Cynergy Bank Emergency Fund	£50.00		
Monzo Spending Account	£80.00						
Credit Cards (Useful)	£	"Bad Debt"	£	Assets	£	Businesses	£
		Sainsbury's Credit	£700.00	Vauxhall Corsa	£4,000.00		
		HSBC Credit Card	£3,000.00				
		Car Finance	£4,500.00				
Savings (Bills/Spendable)	£			Debtors	£	Investments	£
Christmas/Birthday's Fund	£0.00			Rory (Mate)	£80.00		
Yearly Expenses Fund	£0.00						

Spendable Income	£180.00
Liabilities	£8,200.00
Savings, Assets & Debtors	£4,130.00
Investments	£0.00

Net Wealth	-£3,890.00

Lastly, under the **Investment Column**, include any pensions that you have under **Pensions**, any business accounts you have in the **Business Category**, and any other investments- such as a stock and shares ISA- in the **Investment Section**.

Spending Accounts	Value	Liabilities	Value	Saving Accounts & Assets	Value	Investing Accounts	Value
Current Accounts	£	"Good" Debt	£	Savings Accounts	£	Pensions	£
Barclay's Current Account	£100.00			Cynergy Bank Emergency Fund	£50.00	Pension	£15,804.00
Monzo Spending Account	£80.00						
Credit Cards (Useful)	£	"Bad Debt"	£	Assets	£	Businesses	£
		Sainsbury's Credit	£700.00	Vauxhall Corsa	£4,000.00		
		HSBC Credit Card	£3,000.00				
		Car Finance	£4,500.00				
Savings (Bills/Spendable)	£			Debtors	£	Investments	£
Christmas/Birthday's Fund	£0.00			Rory (Mate)	£80.00	Stocks & Shares ISA	£0.00
Yearly Expenses Fund	£0.00						

Spendable Income	£180.00
Liabilities	£8,200.00
Savings, Assets & Debtors	£4,130.00
Investments	£15,804.00

Almost done; remember that I told you to skip the credit card category?

Well, the reason we skipped it is because we want to use this section to log the lines of credit available to us, not to show us the amount we owe.

Having a credit card with no outstanding balance of longer than one month is an extremely useful tool, allowing you to use your **needs** budget which was left in your master account.

To save getting in a muddle with your needs, spending money and bills, you can use a credit card to monitor your needs budget, ensuring that you don't overspend.

For example, Lloyd has a needs budget of **£180**.

Meaning, every time he spends money on a **need**, he uses that credit card.

Then, once his monthly statement comes through, he can pay that off with the money he has left in his bills account. Simple.

The advantage of doing this is that over time, your credit score will increase, opening you up to more opportunities.

However, the catch here is that you must not spend past the amount budgeted for your needs, and you must repay the credit card in full and on time.

Sometimes things may get a bit out of hand, and you might need to overspend. And so, in some cases you might have to move some things about, i.e., reducing a debt repayment, although, ideally reducing your spending money for that month would be a better option.

Here's what your spreadsheet might look like now:

Spending Accounts	Value	Liabilities	Value	Saving Accounts & Assets	Value	Investing Accounts	Value
Current Accounts	£	"Good" Debt	£	Savings Accounts	£	Pensions	£
Barclay's Current Account	£100.00			Cynergy Bank Emergency Fund	£50.00	Pension	£15,804.00
Monzo Spending Account	£80.00						
Credit Cards (Useful)	£	"Bad Debt"	£	Assets	£	Businesses	£
Tesco Credit Card	£0.00	Sainsbury's Credit	£700.00	Vauxhall Corsa	£4,000.00		
		HSBC Credit Card	£3,000.00				
		Car Finance	£4,500.00				
Savings (Bills/Spendable)	£			Debtors	£	Investments	£
Christmas/Birthday's Fund	£0.00			Rory (Mate)	£80.00	Stocks & Shares ISA	£0.00
Yearly Expenses Fund	£0.00						

Spendable Income	£180.00
Liabilities	£8,200.00
Savings, Assets & Debtors	£4,130.00
Investments	£15,804.00
Net Wealth	£11,914.00

The great news for Lloyd is that after finding his pension, and other bits and pieces, his net wealth is no longer negative!

Does this sound stressful? Here's how to automate

The main issue with this technique is, let's be honest, it sounds like a bit of a faff.

Fear not! You only need to set this up once, and you can then sit back and let your bank do the work.

How? Automation.

Here's how it works: Firstly, you need to ensure that your automated monthly expenses come out of your bank account at least **5 days** after your payday, and so make the necessary changes if need be.

Then, create a standing order via your online banking from your master account to your spending account of your allotted spending budget- which should also be scheduled for **5 days** after your payday too.

Why 5 days, you might ask? This gap covers cases where automated payments might be delayed over weekends and bank holidays.

It also gives you a bit of breathing room should you have to make any changes!

Although this might mean your payday comes 5 days later than your colleagues, the bright side is that it helps you build discipline!

If you are debt-free, then you can also create a standing order for money to be paid into your emergency fund and other places too.

Although don't forget to log these funds in the **Red Section** of your **Savings & Investments Column** in your **Monthly Expenses Tab**.

As your number of accounts expands, as should your standing orders.

You now don't need to touch anything, as there will be enough in your account to cover your bills, spending, and saving.

With all of these in place, your job just became a whole lot easier!

All you need to do is spend a few minutes every month updating the **Accounts Tab** to keep on top of the ever-increasing (I should hope) values.

For those of you who tend to get overtime or bonuses, and therefore will have leftover remaining in your master account.

Simply wait until your last bill has come out and distribute the remaining amount in your master account, still leaving the **£100** float.

Overtime/bonuses are great ways to pay off debts sooner and build savings quicker.

Your Maze Checklist

That's it then, the final tasks!

1. Open or reuse some of your existing accounts to create the three-pillars:

A master (bills) account
A spending account
An emergency fund account

Plus, any other specific accounts, you may need.

2. Then close any obsolete accounts you will no longer be needing, after taking the money out of them of course.

3. Now open the **Accounts Tab** on your spreadsheet and fill in everything!

4. Set up the standing orders needed to automate your finances and enjoy your financial journey.

CONCLUSION

As we are on our way out, I'd like to leave you with one golden rule, which I believe, if followed, will offer you a great sense of financial security.

Try to keep your absolute essential bills below what you could earn on minimum wage.

This will lead to being as protected as you can be against any job loss or an unexpected financial downturn.

You'll know that no matter what job you do, you'll be able to keep a roof over your head and food on the table.

Don't get me wrong; I don't mean that all your bills should be below this amount. I'm referring to bills you that you need to pay regardless because they are necessities or that you are contracted in with.

If you are over this amount by your Netflix subscription fee, that's okay. But there's trouble if minimum wage won't be enough to cover your car finance.

I'm talking about the minimum wage as if you lost your job, you can act quickly and get an income coming in, as these types of jobs are the quickest to get.

Many high earners wait around for a few months waiting to seal a similar paying role.

The issue with this is that whilst they are waiting, they are not earning, so they'll be digging into their savings and possibly using credit cards to keep the same lifestyle.

I'm not saying settle for a lower-paying job, but don't turn your nose up at one, you can always look for higher paying jobs in your free time.

As of April 2022, the minimum wage in the UK is **£9.50** for those over 23, meaning if you worked for **38** hours a week, then your post-tax take-home pay would be **£1,564.33** if you're paid monthly, **£1,444** if paid every 4 weeks.

This however might not always be possible if you're living with a partner and or have kids, so what you could both earn earning minimum wage might be a more realistic option.

If you can keep your essential outgoings below this, you'll be okay in a crisis, and if there are really no jobs about... Well then, lucky you've got that emergency fund.

In summary:

Workout your assets and liabilities, understand your pensions and your payslip too.

Focus on reducing unnecessary bills, saving on the musts, and keeping expenditures in check.

Look to repay any bad debt and begin to pay into an emergency fund, separate your accounts, and start to smash your financial targets with the aid of automation.

I'd like to think that you are now well equipped with all the tools to create a solid foundation for your financial life!

This book has taken a lot of time and effort to create, and I hope it has delivered on everything promised on the cover.

With that in mind, if you've found this helpful, then please can you leave a review on Amazon, just here:

Review Link

As it would be extremely helpful in increasing this books reach.

If you feel this hasn't been able to help you as much as you would've liked, I am happy to keep to the promise that I made at the beginning of the book.

Anything you feel that needs improving or could make this book even better, then please discuss with me via email at:

will@the-money-maze.co.uk

This way, you can directly help me in my quest to provide the most complete guide on understanding personal finance in the UK.

Good luck with your finances -

Will

REFERENCES

1. About. (2018, September 28). UNISON National. https://www.unison.org.uk/about/#:%7E:text=With%20more%20than%201.3%20million,services%20and%20for%20utility%20companies

2. Assets. (n.d.). In Bankrate https://www.bankrate.com/glossary/a/assets/#:~:text=What%20are%20assets%3F,may%20generate%20future%20economic%20benefits

3. Baker, N. (2022, March 8). How to switch broadband | A guide to changing your provider. Uswitch. https://www.uswitch.com/broadband/guides/switch/

4. Barrett, S. (2021, August 20). All You Need To Know About How The UK Energy Market Works. Forbes Advisor UK. https://www.forbes.com/uk/advisor/energy/how-the-uk-energy-market-works/

5. Best interest. (n.d.). Money Savings Expert. https://www.moneysavingexpert.com/savings/savings-accounts-best-interest/

6. Car insurance. (n.d.). Money Saving Expert. https://www.moneysavingexpert.com/news/2019/12/car-insurance-optimum-time-to-buy/?_cf_chl_rt_tk=QgAJZmMKQIux6Q5P0I0ICmVNGIU_6z7agSotwg2JPG8-1648158416-0-gaNycGzNCv0

7. Conserving water. (2015, October 5).Ofwat.
https://www.ofwat.gov.uk/households/conservingwater/

8. Council Tax: what it is, what it costs and how to save money | MoneyHelper. (n.d.). MaPS.
https://www.moneyhelper.org.uk/en/homes/buying-a-home/how-to-save-money-on-your-council-tax-bill

9. Credit: What Everyone Should Know. (2022, March 7). Investopedia.
https://www.investopedia.com/terms/c/credit.asp

10. Cut your water bills. (n.d.). Money-Saving Expert.
https://www.moneysavingexpert.com/utilities/cut-water-bills/

11. Debt. (2022, January 13). Investopedia.
https://www.investopedia.com/terms/d/debt.asp

12. Debt Avalanche vs. Debt Snowball: What's the Difference? (2021, April 29). Investopedia.
https://www.investopedia.com/articles/personal-finance/080716/debt-avalanche-vs-debt-snowball-which-best-you.asp

13. Definition and Types of Investments. (2021, August 20). Investopedia.
https://www.investopedia.com/terms/i/investment.asp

14. Direct Debit explained. (n.d.). Direct Debit.
https://www.directdebit.co.uk/DirectDebitExplained/Pages/DirectDebitExplained.aspx

15. Fixed discount mortgage guide. (2022, March 21). Money Saving Expert. https://www.moneysavingexpert.com/mortgages/fixed-discount-mortgage-guide/

16. Full Fact. (n.d.). Fullfact. https://fullfact.org/finder/economy/prices_inflation/

17. Gocardless Team. (2022, March 9). Standing orders: A complete guide. Go Cardless. https://gocardless.com/guides/posts/guide-to-standing-orders/#:%7E:text=A%20standing%20order%20is%20an,choose%20the%20amount%20and%20frequency

18. Good Debt vs. Bad Debt: What's the Difference? (2021, April 29). Investopedia. https://www.investopedia.com/articles/pf/12/good-debt-bad-debt.asp

19. Government Digital Service. (2014a, December 15). National Insurance. GOV.UK. https://www.gov.uk/national-insurance

20. Government Digital Service. (2014b, December 15). National Insurance. GOV.UK. https://www.gov.uk/national-insurance/your-national-insurance-number

21. Government Digital Service. (2014c, December 15). National Insurance. GOV.UK. https://www.gov.uk/national-insurance/national-insurance-classes

22. Government Digital Service. (2014d, December 15). National Insurance. GOV.UK.
https://www.gov.uk/national-insurance/how-much-you-pay

23. Government Digital Service. (2015a, January 26). Workplace pensions. GOV.UK.
https://www.gov.uk/workplace-pensions/joining-a-workplace-pension

24. Government Digital Service. (2015b, January 26). Workplace pensions. GOV.UK.
https://www.gov.uk/workplace-pensions/what-you-your-employer-and-the-government-pay

25. Government Digital Service. (2015c, January 26). Workplace pensions. GOV.UK.
https://www.gov.uk/workplace-pensions/managing-your-pension

26. Government Digital Service. (2015d, April 7). Income Tax rates and Personal Allowances. GOV.UK.
https://www.gov.uk/income-tax-rates

27. Government Digital Service. (2015e, April 15). Tax codes. GOV.UK.
https://www.gov.uk/tax-codes

28. Government Digital Service. (2015f, April 15). Tax codes. GOV.UK.
https://www.gov.uk/tax-codes/what-your-tax-code-means

29. Government Digital Service. (2015g, April 15). Tax codes. GOV.UK.
https://www.gov.uk/tax-codes/emergency-tax-codes

30. Government Digital Service. (2015h, September 15). Tax on your private pension contributions. GOV.UK.
https://www.gov.uk/tax-on-your-private-pension/pension-tax-relief

31. Government Digital Service. (2015i, October 27). Income Tax in Scotland. GOV.UK.
https://www.gov.uk/scottish-income-tax

32. Government Digital Service. (2015j, November 12). Individual Savings Accounts (ISAs). GOV.UK.
https://www.gov.uk/individual-savings-accounts

33. HP vs PCP - Which type of car finance is best for you? (n.d.). Carbase.
https://www.carbase.co.uk/news-and-features/car-finance/hp-vs-pcp-which-type-of-car-finance-is-best/

34. Interest rates and Bank Rate. (2022, March 17). Bank of England.
https://www.bankofengland.co.uk/monetary-policy/the-interest-rate-bank-rate

35. Kiyosaki, R. T. (2017). Rich Dad Poor Dad: What the Rich Teach Their Kids About Money That the Poor and Middle Class Do Not! (Second ed.). Plata Publishing.

36. Liquid Asset. (2021, March 29). Investopedia. https://www.investopedia.com/terms/l/liquidasset.asp#:%7E:text=A%20liquid%20asset%20is%20an,portion%20of%20their%20net%20worth

37. Loan. (2021, April 19). Investopedia. https://www.investopedia.com/terms/l/loan.asp

38. Non-liquid asset. (n.d.). In Bankrate. https://www.bankrate.com/glossary/n/non-liquid-asset/

39. Nurse, F. C. E. (2016, May 6). The "worthless" 100 trillion dollar bank note. CNN. https://edition.cnn.com/2016/05/06/africa/zimbabwe-trillion-dollar-note/index.html

40. Personal loans | MoneyHelper. (n.d.). MaPS. https://www.moneyhelper.org.uk/en/everyday-money/types-of-credit/personal-loans

41. Statista. (2022, January 14). Average monthly grocery basket value in the UK from May 2017 to June 2018. https://www.statista.com/statistics/744906/average-monthly-grocery-basket-value-in-the-united-kingdom/

42. Types of private pensions. (2018, June 11). GOV.UK. https://www.gov.uk/pension-types

43. Understanding Depreciation. (2022, March 9). Investopedia. https://www.investopedia.com/terms/d/depreciation.asp

44. Understanding How Interest Works. (2022a, January 7). Investopedia. https://www.investopedia.com/terms/i/interest.asp#:%7E:text=Interest%20is%20the%20monetary%20charge,receives%20for%20lending%20out%20money

45. Understanding How Interest Works. (2022b, January 7). Investopedia. https://www.investopedia.com/terms/i/interest.asp

46. Understanding Taxes. (2021, October 14). Investopedia. https://www.investopedia.com/terms/t/taxes.asp

47. What Is a Liability? (2021, September 10). Investopedia. https://www.investopedia.com/terms/l/liability.asp

48. What is a prepayment energy tariff? (n.d.). Uk Power. https://www.ukpower.co.uk/home_energy/bill-payment-methods

49. What is an asset? (2022, January 28). Investopedia. https://www.investopedia.com/terms/a/asset.asp

50. What Is Base Pay? (2021, December 8). Investopedia. https://www.investopedia.com/terms/b/base-pay.asp

51. What Is Negative Equity? (2021, February 19). Investopedia. https://www.investopedia.com/terms/n/negativeequity.asp

52. When can I switch energy suppliers without a penalty? (2022, February 16). Utility Bidder. https://www.utilitybidder.co.uk/domestic-energy/when-can-i-switch-energy-suppliers-without-a%20penalty/#:%7E:text=Introduced%20by%20Ofgem%2C%20the%20window,best%20time%20to%20swap%20providers

NOTES

NOTES

NOTES

NOTES

NOTES

NOTES

NOTES

NOTES

NOTES

NOTES

Printed in Great Britain
by Amazon